Greenhaven

$20.96

P.O. 67128

HATE GROUPS

OPPOSING VIEWPOINTS®

OTHER BOOKS OF RELATED INTEREST

OPPOSING VIEWPOINTS SERIES

Crime and Criminals
Culture Wars
Discrimination
Gangs
Interracial America
Race Relations
Violence

CURRENT CONTROVERSIES SERIES

Crime
Gay Rights
Hate Crimes
Minorities
Racism
Urban Terrorism
Youth Violence

AT ISSUE SERIES

Anti-Semitism
Ethnic Conflict

HATE GROUPS

OPPOSING VIEWPOINTS®

Tamara L. Roleff, *Book Editor*
Brenda Stalcup, *Assistant Editor*
Mary E. Williams, *Assistant Editor*

David L. Bender, *Publisher*
Bruno Leone, *Executive Editor*
Bonnie Szumski, *Editorial Director*
Brenda Stalcup, *Managing Editor*
Scott Barbour, *Senior Editor*

OPPOSING
VIEWPOINTS®
SERIES

Greenhaven Press, Inc., San Diego, California

Library of Congress Cataloging-in-Publication Data

Hate groups : opposing viewpoints / Tamara L. Roleff, book editor.
 Brenda Stalcup, Mary E. Williams, assistant editors.
    p.   cm. — (Opposing viewpoints series)
  Includes bibliographical references and index.
  ISBN 1-56510-943-0 (lib. bdg. : alk. paper). —
ISBN 1-56510-942-2 (pbk. : alk. paper)
    1. Hate crimes—United States. 2. Hate crimes—Moral and ethical
aspects—United States. 3. Hate crimes—Government policy—United
States. 4. Hate groups—United States. 5. Militia movements—United
States. I. Stalcup, Brenda. II. Roleff, Tamara L., 1959–   . III. Williams,
Mary E., 1960–   . IV. Series: Opposing viewpoints series
(Unnumbered)
HV6773.52.H37 1999
364.1—dc21   98-36586
                                                                            CIP

Greenhaven Press, Inc., P.O. Box 289009
San Diego, CA 92198-9009

"CONGRESS SHALL MAKE NO LAW...ABRIDGING THE FREEDOM OF SPEECH, OR OF THE PRESS."

First Amendment to the U.S. Constitution

The basic foundation of our democracy is the First Amendment guarantee of freedom of expression. The Opposing Viewpoints Series is dedicated to the concept of this basic freedom and the idea that it is more important to practice it than to enshrine it.

CONTENTS

WHY CONSIDER
OPPOSING VIEWPOINTS?

"The only way in which a human being can make some approach to knowing the whole of a subject is by hearing what can be said about it by persons of every variety of opinion and studying all modes in which it can be looked at by every character of mind. No wise man ever acquired his wisdom in any mode but this."

John Stuart Mill

In our media-intensive culture it is not difficult to find differing opinions. Thousands of newspapers and magazines and dozens of radio and television talk shows resound with differing points of view. The difficulty lies in deciding which opinion to agree with and which "experts" seem the most credible. The more inundated we become with differing opinions and claims, the more essential it is to hone critical reading and thinking skills to evaluate these ideas. Opposing Viewpoints books address this problem directly by presenting stimulating debates that can be used to enhance and teach these skills. The varied opinions contained in each book examine many different aspects of a single issue. While examining these conveniently edited opposing views, readers can develop critical thinking skills such as the ability to compare and contrast authors' credibility, facts, argumentation styles, use of persuasive techniques, and other stylistic tools. In short, the Opposing Viewpoints Series is an ideal way to attain the higher-level thinking and reading skills so essential in a culture of diverse and contradictory opinions.

In addition to providing a tool for critical thinking, Opposing Viewpoints books challenge readers to question their own strongly held opinions and assumptions. Most people form their opinions on the basis of upbringing, peer pressure, and personal, cultural, or professional bias. By reading carefully balanced opposing views, readers must directly confront new ideas as well as the opinions of those with whom they disagree. This is not to simplistically argue that everyone who reads opposing views will—or should—change his or her opinion. Instead, the series enhances readers' understanding of their own views by encouraging confrontation with opposing ideas. Careful examination of others' views can lead to the readers' understanding of the logical inconsistencies in their own opinions, perspective on why they hold an opinion, and the consideration of the possibility that their opinion requires further evaluation.

EVALUATING OTHER OPINIONS

To ensure that this type of examination occurs, Opposing Viewpoints books present all types of opinions. Prominent spokespeople on different sides of each issue as well as well-known professionals from many disciplines challenge the reader. An additional goal of the series is to provide a forum for other, less known, or even unpopular viewpoints. The opinion of an ordinary person who has had to make the decision to cut off life support from a terminally ill relative, for example, may be just as valuable and provide just as much insight as a medical ethicist's professional opinion. The editors have two additional purposes in including these less known views. One, the editors encourage readers to respect others' opinions—even when not enhanced by professional credibility. It is only by reading or listening to and objectively evaluating others' ideas that one can determine whether they are worthy of consideration. Two, the inclusion of such viewpoints encourages the important critical thinking skill of objectively evaluating an author's credentials and bias. This evaluation will illuminate an author's reasons for taking a particular stance on an issue and will aid in readers' evaluation of the author's ideas.

As series editors of the Opposing Viewpoints Series, it is our hope that these books will give readers a deeper understanding of the issues debated and an appreciation of the complexity of even seemingly simple issues when good and honest people disagree. This awareness is particularly important in a democratic society such as ours in which people enter into public debate to determine the common good. Those with whom one disagrees should not be regarded as enemies but rather as people whose views deserve careful examination and may shed light on one's own.

Thomas Jefferson once said that "difference of opinion leads to inquiry, and inquiry to truth." Jefferson, a broadly educated man, argued that "if a nation expects to be ignorant and free . . . it expects what never was and never will be." As individuals and as a nation, it is imperative that we consider the opinions of others and examine them with skill and discernment. The Opposing Viewpoints Series is intended to help readers achieve this goal.

David L. Bender & Bruno Leone,
Series Editors

Greenhaven Press anthologies primarily consist of previously published material taken from a variety of sources, including periodicals, books, scholarly journals, newspapers, government documents, and position papers from private and public organizations. These original sources are often edited for length and to ensure their accessibility for a young adult audience. The anthology editors also change the original titles of these works in order to clearly present the main thesis of each viewpoint and to explicitly indicate the opinion presented in the viewpoint. These alterations are made in consideration of both the reading and comprehension levels of a young adult audience. Every effort is made to ensure that Greenhaven Press accurately reflects the original intent of the authors included in this anthology.

INTRODUCTION

> "If you join a pro-white group that promotes the history, heritage, or culture of the white race, you are given thumbs down and called a hater and a racist."
> —Charles Lee, Grand Dragon of the Knights of the White Kamellia, Ku Klux Klan, in Soldiers of God, 1998

> "Hate groups can spawn violence even when they do not directly participate in the crimes."
> —Morris Dees and Ellen Bowden, Trial, February 1995

Mulugeta Seraw, an Ethiopian immigrant, was killed by three white skinheads in Portland, Oregon, in November 1988. Two years later, Tom Metzger, leader of the White Aryan Resistance (WAR), and his son John were found liable for Seraw's murder in a civil suit because they recruited the skinheads and encouraged them to participate in violent behavior against nonwhites. In Fayetteville, North Carolina, James Burmeister, a soldier and self-described skinhead, shot and killed a couple out walking one night in December 1995 "because they were black." In June 1998 in Jasper, Texas, three men with ties to a white supremacist group chained James Byrd Jr. by his ankles and dragged him behind a pickup truck until his body literally fell apart. He was killed, said one of the men involved, because the truck's driver did not like blacks.

Because of their racial overtones, these murders have drawn the public's attention to white supremacist organizations such as the Ku Klux Klan, WAR, Aryan Nations, Christian Patriots, and various skinhead groups. The groups' members contend that while they believe in the supremacy of the white race and the separation of the races, they do not condone acts of violence—especially murder—against nonwhites. The criminals who commit these crimes are the exception to the law-abiding citizens who comprise these groups, they assert. Hate crimes studies appear to support their contention, showing that most hate crimes are committed by individuals acting on their own.

Members of white supremacist groups claim that they are misunderstood by the public, and that they themselves are the victims of religious persecution. They do not hate nonwhites, they assert, but are only following their religious beliefs—based on the Bible—that decree that the races must be kept separate.

Their politically incorrect beliefs lead to persecution, charges Jim Stinson, a Knight of the White Kamellia, Ku Klux Klan of Texas:

> You know there are all kinds of good Christians out there. They don't hate anyone, right? That is, they don't hate anyone but us. We believe in our race and our God and we don't back away from that. That makes us the bad guys, the racists. It's open season on us.

White supremacists contend that this "open season" includes harassment by law enforcement officers and others at their rallies, meetings, and marches. In addition, supporters of white supremacist groups maintain that their religious beliefs are singled out for abuse while practitioners of other unusual religions are allowed to practice their beliefs in peace. For example, some point out that the use of peyote, an illegal drug, is permitted during religious ceremonies performed by Native Americans, and doctors respect the beliefs of Jehovah's Witnesses and Christian Scientists who refuse blood transfusions or other medical treatments. However, they assert, white supremacists are not allowed to follow their religious beliefs concerning racial separation and white supremacy.

Many white supremacists also resent being forced to support welfare recipients with tax dollars, accept homosexuality as an alternative lifestyle, and permit legalized abortion, all of which, they argue, are mandated by the government and contradict their beliefs. These groups see themselves as defenders of traditional American values that are under attack by the government.

Critics of white supremacists do not see them as victims of persecution but rather as the persecutors. White supremacists are racists, they contend, and their beliefs are based on hate, not religion. Hate crimes observers blame organizations such as WAR, Aryan Nations, and Christian Patriots for many of the hate crimes committed, even if they are committed by people unconnected with the groups. According to hate crimes experts Jack Levin and Jack McDevitt, skinheads and violent racists rely on WAR, Aryan Nations, and similar groups for guidance and encouragement in acting out their aggression and resentment against nonwhites and other "undesirables." Furthermore, they contend, organizations such as WAR have a pervasive influence on alienated teenagers and young adults. These youths see themselves as helping the white supremacist groups carry out their mission of "ridding the United States, if not the world, of its 'subhuman' residents," Levin and McDevitt write.

Due to the pervasive influence of political correctness, however, racism is less effective than it once was for attracting new members to hate groups, according to Loretta Ross, program research director at the hate crimes watch group Center for Democratic Renewal. She contends that hostility toward the government seems to rally more new members to hate groups than racism or anti-Semitism. A central theme of the extremists' antigovernment rhetoric is that the federal government is trying to restrict as many rights of the people as it can. While the views of hate group members may be harmless in and of themselves, hate crimes observers note that the extremists speak of using violence to prevent the behaviors of which they disapprove—such as abortion and homosexuality—from being tolerated or accepted. The intended subjects of these proposed and actual armed assaults are usually federal officials, law enforcement officers, abortion providers and clinics, environmentalists, minorities, gays and lesbians, Jews, and welfare recipients. According to authors Chip Berlet and Matthew N. Lyons, white supremacists believe these groups all represent a threat in some way or another to maintaining the rights and privileges of the white race.

The debate over whether certain organizations violate individuals' civil rights when they act out or verbalize their hate toward specific people or whether these groups are simply protecting their right to live according to their beliefs is the subject of *Hate Groups: Opposing Viewpoints*. The authors explore hate crimes and hate groups in the following chapters: Are Hate Crimes a Serious Problem? Do Certain Groups Promote Hate and Violence? Does the Militia Movement Present a Serious Threat? How Can Hate Crimes and Terrorism Be Reduced? The viewpoints in this anthology examine whether hate groups constitute a danger to America.

CHAPTER 1

ARE HATE CRIMES A SERIOUS PROBLEM?

Chapter Preface

In the spring and early summer of 1996, newspapers, magazines, and television newscasts featured pictures of burning churches along with headlines such as "Burning Hate" and "Terror in the Night Down South." The stories told of an increasing number of arsons at churches, especially black churches, in the South. Each time another church burned, the number of stories in the media about church arsons increased exponentially, with many authors theorizing that a conspiracy by white racists was responsible for the fires. Chief among the proponents of this theory was the Center for Democratic Renewal, a hate crimes watch group that was monitoring the fires. The CDR announced at a March 1996 press conference that ninety black churches had been burned in nine southern states since 1990 and that more were being burned every year. By mid-summer 1996, however, a few voices began to claim that the "epidemic" of black church arsons was a hoax.

One of the leading critics of the church arson stories was Michael Fumento, an editor at *Reason* magazine. He argued that in states that kept records going back to 1990, the number of fires at black churches in 1994 and 1995 was less than in 1990 and 1991. Moreover, Fumento maintained, many of the fires that were characterized as arsons by the CDR were not labeled as arson by the investigating law enforcement agency. Furthermore, he asserted, a significant number of the arson fires at black churches were set by blacks, not by racist whites.

Despite Fumento's protestations, the CDR insisted that its numbers for black church arsons was accurate, or even perhaps too low. Many small, black churches are poor, the CDR maintains, and are unlikely to be insured. Therefore, the center argued, these churches would not be included in statistics compiled by the insurance industry on arsons. Moreover, the CDR asserted, the fact that states are not required to file their arson reports with the federal government also contributed to a low and inaccurate count of black church arsons.

The controversy over the black church-burning epidemic mirrors the arguments over other hate crimes. Some contend that such crimes are a serious problem, while others believe their prevalence is exaggerated by the media. This and other issues are examined in the following chapter on the severity of hate crimes.

"From killings and beatings to acts of
arson and vandalism, these hate
crimes injure or even kill thousands
of people, terrify countless others,
divide Americans against each other,
and distort our entire society."

HATE CRIMES ARE A SERIOUS PROBLEM

Karen McGill Lawson and Wade Henderson

In the following viewpoint, Karen McGill Lawson and Wade Henderson argue that the number of hate crime victims in America is widely underreported and that the high incidence of hate crimes is a national emergency that requires immediate action. The most frequent victims of hate crimes are racial minorities, they assert, although victims are also targeted based on their ethnicity, religion, and sexual orientation. Because the perpetrators of these crimes are motivated by hate, the authors maintain, the victims are much more likely to be seriously assaulted and require hospitalization. Lawson is the executive director of the Leadership Conference Educational Fund, a research organization established to support educational activities related to civil rights. Henderson is the executive director of the Leadership Conference on Civil Rights, the nation's largest coalition of civil rights and labor groups.

As you read, consider the following questions:

1. What was the first step America's leaders took in recognizing the urgency of the problem of hate crimes, according to the authors?
2. How does the Hate Crimes Statistics Act define hate crimes, as cited by Lawson and Henderson?

Reprinted, by permission, from Leadership Conference Education Fund/Leadership Conference on Civil Rights, *Cause for Concern: Hate Crimes in America*, Karen McGill Lawson, Exec. Dir. LCEF, and Wade Henderson, Exec. Dir. LCCR, Washington, D.C., January 1997.

Just around the holiday season, in December 1994, a flyer was tacked to the door of the Macedonia Baptist Church in Bloomville, South Carolina. The message on the door of this African-American church was at odds with the Christmas spirit of peace and good will: It was an announcement of a Ku Klux Klan rally.

Six months later, after nightfall on June 20, 1995, the Macedonia Baptist Church was burned to the ground. Earlier that same morning, another African-American church, the Mount Zion AME Church in nearby Greelyville, S.C., had also burned to the ground.

Local police arrested two young white men, Christopher Cox, 22, and Timothy Adron Welch, 23, in connection with the fires. The county sheriff, Hoyt Collins, said Welch was carrying a membership card for the Christian Knights of the Ku Klux Klan, one of the most active white supremacist groups in the state, when he was arrested.

Indicted for arson under state law, Cox and Welch have pleaded guilty and are awaiting sentencing. Meanwhile, two former Klansmen who federal authorities say masterminded the burning of the predominately black church in Bloomville were indicted recently on civil rights violations. The indictment also charges the two men with burning a Hispanic migrant camp in Manning, S.C. And the FBI is investigating the possibility that the fires at these two churches in Clarendon County, S.C., are linked to fires at other African-American houses of worship throughout the country.

AN EVEN BIGGER PROBLEM

From January 1, 1995, through June 27, 1996, there were 73 suspicious fires or acts of desecration at African-American churches. For African-Americans and all Americans of good will, this wave of church burnings has prompted outrage and alarm. And it is awakening bitter memories of racist violence during the civil rights struggle—particularly the 1963 bombing of the Sixth Street Baptist Church in Birmingham, Alabama, that killed four young girls.

Appalling as it is, however, the searing image of burning churches stands for an even larger problem: the persistence of violent crimes against virtually every racial, ethnic, religious, and sexual minority, as well as against women. The reaction of some to recent controversies over immigration, welfare, and the languages spoken in public places—issues that go to the heart of America's identity as a caring, diverse and inclusive society—has increased the incidence of hate crimes against Hispanics, Asian-Pacific Americans, and others who are stereotyped, often inaccurately, as newcomers to this country. And the persistence of religious, ethnic, and sexual intolerance creates and contributes to a climate where hate crimes are perpetrated against Jews, Arab-Americans, gays and lesbians, women and members of other groups at risk of attack.

SYMPTOM OF A LARGER EVIL

From killings and beatings to acts of arson and vandalism, these hate crimes injure or even kill thousands of people, terrify countless others, divide Americans against each other, and distort our entire society.

To be sure, hate crimes are symptoms of a host of social ills. For all the progress our nation has made in civil and human rights, bigotry in all its forms dies hard. And discrimination is a continuing reality in many areas of American life, including the workplace. . . .

HATE CRIMES ARE INCREASING

Although some violent crimes are decreasing, hate crimes and arsons are increasing. Extremist movements are gaining in numbers and prominence, and their targets range from minority groups to the government itself. Public debate over social policy issues—from affirmative action to immigration to welfare—unfortunately is used by public officials to divide us from one another. Social problems of all kinds are exacerbated by the economic anxieties prompted by corporate downsizing, stagnant wages, and vanishing health coverage and pension benefits. In such an environment, hate crimes persist as expressions of hatred, alienation, and an effort to intimidate and demean those perceived as a threat to one's own status.

It is often the case that symptoms themselves must be treated before illnesses can be cured. Hate crimes are a national emergency requiring national action.

Our nation's leaders took an initial step in recognizing the urgency of the problem with the passage in 1990 of the Hate Crime Statistics Act (HCSA) and its reauthorization in 1996. It requires the Department of Justice to compile data on crimes that "manifest prejudice based on race, religion, sexual orientation, or ethnicity" and to publish an annual summary of the findings. The law helps local, state, and national law enforcement authorities coordinate their efforts against hate crimes. And its very existence makes a powerful statement that the United States of America celebrates the diversity of its people—and will not tolerate violent acts of intolerance.

Six years after the initial enactment of this law, it is even more urgent for Americans to work together against the epidemic of ultra-violent behavior motivated by bigotry. . . .

We believe that hate crimes are a more serious problem than is generally recognized. And we maintain that this problem requires a unified and determined response by national and state leaders in government and business, by law enforcement agencies at every level, by civic, religious, and educational organizations of all kinds, and by ordinary citizens in their communities, on their jobs, in their houses of worship, and in their schools.

Once and for all, now and forever, it is time to extinguish the flames of hatred in America.

The federal government's definition of hate crimes—and its annual reports on total reported incidents—paint only a partial portrait of the problem.

THE CRIMES

The Hate Crime Statistics Act defines hate crimes as acts in which individuals are victimized because of their "race, religion, sexual orientation, or ethnicity." This definition fails to convey a deeper sense of the severity of hate crimes or their impact on individual victims, their families and communities, and our country. Nor does it address hate crimes against women simply because they are women. The definition in the federal Hate Crimes Sentencing Enhancement Act of 1994, includes women and persons with disabilities. In this statute, hate crimes are those in which "the defendant intentionally selects a victim, or in the case of a property crime, the property that is the object of the crime, because of the actual or perceived race, color, religion, national origin, ethnicity, gender, disability, or sexual orientation of any person."

In 1993, the Supreme Court upheld the constitutionality of Wisconsin's hate crime statute, which enhances the sentence of crimes in which the perpetrator "intentionally selects" the victim "because of" his or her characteristics. The Wisconsin law was carefully written not to punish a person's prejudicial opinions, but rather to punish criminal intent and conduct.

Hate crimes are much more likely than other crimes to be acts of brutal violence. In comparison to other crimes, targets of hate violence are singled out because of their membership in a social group. Perpetrators are more likely to be marauding groups of predators looking for targets for their hatred. However, they can also be acquaintances, intimate partners or family members. Because the intention is to hurt, maim, or kill, hate-motivated crimes are five times as likely as other crimes to involve assault. And these assaults are twice as likely as other assaults to cause injury and to result in hospitalization.

HATE CRIMES BY CATEGORY, 1995

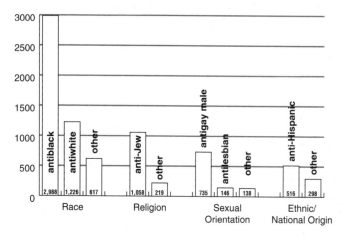

Source: Karen McGill Lawson and Wade Henderson, *Cause for Concern: Hate Crimes in America,* 1997.

Thus, the individual victim of a hate crime is more likely to be severely injured in body, and in spirit as well, than the victim of an ordinary offense. Unlike someone who is robbed of a wallet, someone who is attacked for no reason except their membership in a targeted class is more likely to be beaten out of sheer cruelty. And while crime victims often ask, "Why me?" the answers are perhaps more hurtful for victims of hate crimes. Victims of hate crimes experience psychic pain regardless of the motivation of the crime. However, it is one thing to be victimized for walking down a deserted street or wearing an expensive wristwatch; but it is perhaps more painful to be victimized simply for who you are. The cruelty of these crimes is magnified because they remind the victims of terrible things that had been done in the past to members of their group, or to them, their families, or their friends—pogroms against Jews, lynchings of blacks, rapes and beatings of women, lesbians and gay men, or grim memories in the minds of other groups.

As for the communities hit by hate crimes, these incidents make targeted individuals feel even more angry and alienated, increasing intergroup tensions of all kinds. Because victims are singled out because of who they are—and the targets of hate crimes are often community institutions such as synagogues or black churches—members of entire groups feel isolated and defenseless. Others, such as a survivor of domestic violence, must live with the fear and isolation of ongoing assaults. Rightly or wrongly, they often blame the police, the government, and other segments of society for their feelings of vulnerability. Sometimes, members of the groups that have been victimized lash out against members of other groups. Thus, hate crimes can set in motion a never-ending spiral of antagonism and divisiveness.

THE VICTIMS

Official statistics illuminate—but greatly understate—the scope of the problem.

As required by the 1990 law, the Federal Bureau of Investigation (FBI) releases the totals each year for the numbers of hate crimes reported by state and local law enforcement agencies around the country based on race, religion, sexual orientation or ethnicity. These national totals have fluctuated around 6,000 or more hate crimes reported each year—6,918 in 1992, 7,587 in 1993, 5,852 in 1994 and 7,947 in 1995. It should be noted that these are figures for "incidents." The same incident may include several different "offenses"—for instance, an arson or assault may also result in death.

While more than 25,000 hate crimes reported in four years are alarming enough, the FBI statistics paint only a partial portrait of the problem. In 1994, for instance, the total number of law enforcement agencies that reported hate crimes to the FBI covered only 58% of the population of the United States. In 1995, the number of reporting agencies covered 75% of the population. The findings reflect only those cases where the victims reported incidents to local law enforcement agencies, and these agencies had classified these incidents as hate crimes. In 1995, the FBI reported 355 incidents of hate crimes against Asian Pacific Islanders. For the same year, the National Asian Pacific American Legal Consortium's 1995 audit reported 458 incidents of hateful speech and hate crimes, and concluded that "anti-Asian violence is widely underreported." Further, the FBI collects no statistics on gender-based hate crimes, and its definition may exclude other forms of bias crimes such as attacks on Arab-Americans.

Yet even these incomplete statistics suggest the scope and sweep of the problem. Thus, of the 7,947 total incidents and 9,895 total offenses reported in 1995, there were 7,144 crimes against persons. These crimes included 4,048 acts of intimidation, 1,796 simple assaults, 1,268 aggravated assaults, 20 murders and 12 forcible rapes. Sixty percent of the incidents were motivated by racial bias, 16 percent by religious bias, 13 percent by sexual-orientation bias, and 10 percent by bias against the victims' ethnicity or national origin. All in all, there were 10,469 victims and 8,433 known offenders, not including offenses against women as a class.

THE ATTACKERS

As for the perpetrators of hate crimes, a surprisingly large number may be youthful thrill-seekers, rather than hardcore haters. According to a study conducted in 1993 for Northeastern University, 60% of offenders committed crimes for the "thrill associated with the victimization." Often, the perpetrators hoped their acts of violence would gain respect from their friends—a feeling that explains why so many hate crimes are committed by gangs of young men. As one young "gaybasher" explained: "We were trying to be tough to each other. It was like a game of chicken—someone dared you to do something, and there was no backing down."

The second most common perpetrator of hate crimes, reported under the act is the "reactive offender" who feels that he's answering an attack by his victim—a perceived insult, interracial dating, the integration of his neighborhood, or his battered wife's decision to leave. Often, the "reactive offenders" imagine that the very existence of lesbians and gay men—or having to compete with women on the job—is an assault upon their values or their own identity.

The least common offender reported under the act, is the hard-core fanatic, imbued with the ideology of racial, religious, or ethnic bigotry and often a member of, or a potential recruit for, an extremist organization. While the oldest organized hate groups appear to be on the decline, new strategies are emerging where organized hatemongers incite impressionable individuals to commit acts of violence against targeted minorities.

"There are many whiners and losers
. . . who are bright enough to figure
out that one sure way to get
sympathy and attention . . . is to
become the latest victim of big, bad
'White racism.'"

MANY HATE CRIMES ARE HOAXES

Kevin Alfred Strom

Kevin Alfred Strom argues in the following viewpoint that many
"hate crimes" are hoaxes that are committed by members of the
race that is allegedly being persecuted. These perpetrators commit these fraudulent hate crimes to receive attention, money,
and even celebrity, he maintains. When the hate crime hoaxers
are caught, he contends, they are rarely punished as severely as
white perpetrators of such crimes would be. Strom is the host of
the radio program *American Dissident Voices*, which is sponsored by
the National Alliance, an organization that promotes the advancement and protection of the white race.

As you read, consider the following questions:

1. According to Strom, who benefits from the hate crime
   hoaxes?
2. In Strom's opinion, why do the elite embrace the hysteria
   associated with racism and hate crimes?
3. According to the author, who are the only ones who are
   capable of stopping the hoaxers?

Reprinted from Kevin Alfred Strom, "A-Hoaxing We Will Go," *Free Speech*, July 1996, by
permission of *Free Speech*, PO Box 330, Hillsboro, WV 24946; www.natvan.com.

et me make a comment or two about fires in Black churches. If there is—and I doubt that there is—but if there is anyone out there who thinks that he is on my side who is setting fire to the places of worship of churchgoing Blacks, such a person does more to hurt the cause of White separatism than ten Simon Wiesenthals. Such a person is not on my side. The fact that these arsons serve so splendidly the "anti-racist" cause should give one pause to think "cui bono?"—who benefits?

Let's examine a few specific cases while we keep that important question in mind.

ANTI-ASIAN HOAX

In November, 1990, 150 University of Washington students joined in an "anti-racism" rally. Chanting, "Hey ho, hey ho, racism has got to go," carrying banners and marching on the office of the university's president, they demanded that "justice be done" in the case of a racially motivated attack by Whites on an Asian student named Darres Park.

According to Park, he and two White friends had been minding their own business one day in October, when Park had been set upon by three Whites wielding tire irons and baseball bats. The White attackers held off Park's friends, while a crowd of racist Whites gathered and cheered the attackers on, some chanting, "Brain the gook!" According to Park, if it weren't for his knowledge of the martial arts, the "racists" might have been successful in killing him.

Darres Park became a national hero in the "anti-racist" crusade, attracting media attention around the nation and even getting a mention in the *International Herald Examiner*.

Then his story started to unravel, as did his reputation.

Seattle police were stunned by the ferocity of accusations by Park and his "anti-racist" cheering section that police had bungled the investigation of this "hate crime." So law enforcement officials stepped up their investigation of all the personalities and circumstances surrounding this alleged incident. They discovered that a friend of Park's, who supposedly had been with him when the initial report of the attack was made, now claimed that no such report was ever given to police. Secondly, it was discovered that Park's wrist had never been broken as he had claimed. Inquiries among Park's fellow students revealed that very few of them believed Park's story, and most had doubted it from the very beginning.

Further investigation revealed that Park may have been trying to create "victim status" for himself to get public sympathy. He was going to need all the public sympathy he could get, since the Seattle police subsequently discovered evidence leading them, on December 13, 1990, to charge Darres Park with three armed bank robberies in Seattle and Battle Ground, Washington. Charged along with Park, as accomplice in the bank robberies, was Joseph Fritz, one of Park's "White friends" who supposedly "witnessed" the attack and supported Park's claims in statements to police.

Perhaps the wildest statement to emerge from the Park affair was one by Darres Park's defense lawyer in the bank robbery case, Robert Leen, who said that Park may have robbed the banks because of brain damage sustained in the "racial assault."

Cui bono? Who benefits?

ANTI-SEMITIC FRAUD

In the predominantly Jewish neighborhoods of Borough Park and Flatbush in Brooklyn, New York, rocks were thrown through windows of eight Jewish-owned shops. News media across the nation reacted with alarm, comparing the incidents to "Nazi atrocities" and calling for increased vigilance against "anti-Semitism." Jewish pressure groups demanded and got increased police patrols in their neighborhoods. The Jewish mayor of New York City at the time, Ed Koch, offered a $10,000 reward for the perpetrator. The Jewish Community Relations Council offered a $5,000 reward.

Finally, the police made an arrest in the case, and charged the suspect with 14 counts of felonies and misdemeanors relating to this supposed "hate crime."

The arrestee was a 38-year-old Jew named Gary Dworkin. As in most such cases, it was alleged by the Jewish community that Dworkin was mentally ill and deserved more sympathy than punishment.

Cui bono? Who benefits?

THE DANGERS OF ANTI-SEMITISM

In Hartford, Connecticut, suspicious fires occurred at two synagogues and at the homes of Rabbi Solomon Krupka and Jewish State Representative Joan Kemler. Again comparisons were made in the media to "Nazi" terrorism against Jews in Germany.

All across the nation, legislatures were lobbied for passage of "hate crime" laws, with the supposedly "anti-Semitic" fires in Hartford being a focus of concern. Armed Jewish Defense League thugs patrolled the streets of West Hartford. Police staked out whole square blocks and waited for another incident to occur.

Finally, the police had their suspect and his confession to all four arsons. The perpetrator was none other than Barry Dov Schuss, a 17-year-old Jewish student, who had confessed to Rabbi Krupka days before he told the truth to police. If a real "anti-Semite" had been apprehended and convicted, the total sentence could have amounted to virtually life in prison. But Schuss was a good Jewish boy. Schuss stated to all who would listen that he had been an avid reader of literature on the "Holocaust," and freely admitted that he had set the fires to awaken the public to the dangers of "anti-Semitism." Schuss received a suspended sentence, probation, and the ubiquitous—in these cases—psychiatric treatment.

Cui bono? Who benefits?

THE GREAT BLACK CHURCH-BURNING HOAX

"Flames of Hate: Racism Blamed in Shock Wave of Church Burnings," screamed the headline in the New York Daily News. "A Southern Plague Returns," cried another in Virginia that same day.

And who is to blame? . . .

President Bill Clinton, whom critics have accused of taking political advantage of the crisis, proclaimed that "Racial hostility is the driving force" behind the church burnings and said, "I want to ask every citizen in America to say we are not going back, we are not slipping back to those dark days."

Okay, Mr. President, I'll say it. I'll say it because this "epidemic of hatred" is a fraud. A myth. Indeed, a deliberate hoax. There is no good evidence of any increase in black church burnings in the south or anywhere else.

Michael Fumento, July 9, 1996, www.consumeralert.org/fumento/arson.htm.

In New York City there is a large housing cooperative called Co-op City. The residents there were shocked to discover the presence of "anti-Semitic" graffiti and swastikas "daubed" on the doors and walls of 51 different apartments.

Once again the "anti-racist" publicity machine went into action, and the spray-painting incident was publicized widely as another incident of "racism" and "hate." A $3,500 reward was offered for information leading to the apprehension of the "racists."

Subsequently two Jewish youths were charged with the vandalism, after it had been determined that they lied to police and had also tried to collect the reward money by turning in someone else. According to police, these same Jews are also suspected of several other "racist" and "anti-Semitic" incidents which had been publicly attributed to "racists."

Cui bono? Who benefits?

In Basel, Switzerland, local Jews were frightened by an ongoing campaign of anti-Jewish graffiti, harassment, and death threats. Police investigation revealed that the sole culprit in these incidents was a 23-year-old Jewish medical student named Philip Gotchel, member of a prominent Jewish family in the area. If Gotchel had not been discovered, who would have been blamed for these incidents?

Cui bono? Who benefits?

DESPERATE FOR PUBLICITY

You may remember the case of the phony populist TV talk host Morton Downey, Jr. Downey, while he is not as far as I know Jewish, is a rabid "anti-racist." In this incident, Downey, desperate for publicity and to prove his suffering for the "anti-racist" cause, claimed to have been attacked by "racist skinheads" in a San Francisco Airport restroom. Patches of hair were torn from his scalp and a swastika was painted on his face, though some early reports had it that it was "carved" on his face. Later the same day, Downey appeared on television with a much larger swastika painted on his face than when he originally reported the incident. He emotionally detailed his suffering at the hands of the "racists." Witnesses in the restroom and security personnel stationed near the door reported nothing unusual at the time that Downey claimed he was attacked. The police investigators declared the entire incident to be a fabrication and a hoax. Though Downey never admitted his lies, he later stated that he was "drunk" at the time and no longer remembered the attack.

Cui bono? Who benefits?

COVERING UP AN EMBEZZLEMENT

In San Leandro, California, a Black church, the Manor Baptist Church, was aflame, smoke pouring from its offices and library. Investigators smelled both kerosene and gasoline in the ruins—almost certain signs of arson. When they found "racist" graffiti in the church, they were sure: "What we have here is a hate crime," stated police Lt. James O'Meara. But what they had there wasn't anything of the kind, as it turned out. It turns out that a deacon of the church, Brother Shawn Ragan, who was also the former principal of the church school and treasurer, had embezzled some $20,000 from the church and had lit the fire to cover his tracks. When confronted with the truth, Brother Shawn admitted: "I sprayed the graffiti to make them think the arson was racially motivated."

Cui bono? Who benefits? . . .

THE CRIMES ARE FANTASTIC INVENTIONS

Who benefits, indeed? The fight to stamp out "racism" shares many characteristics with the fight to stamp out witchcraft of three hundred years ago. The image in the popular mind of the "evil ones" is almost entirely fictional. The crimes the evil ones are accused of committing are often found to be nonexistent, or fantastic inventions, or incredible inversions of reality. If you are accused of being an evil one, a fair trial is impossible no matter what the actual charge. Accusations of being an evil one are a sure way to destroy business or political rivals.

The ruling elites embrace the hysteria with open arms, for it harnesses the fears and ignorance of the mob to destroy any and all whom the elites want to destroy, without the necessity for messy things like proof or an appearance of fairness. The passions of the boobs can of course be manipulated with much more precision in our age of all-embracing media than they could three centuries ago. Joe Sixpack will, without too much prompting, call for or at least acquiesce in the lynching of whomever his television set declares a "racist."

So a-hoaxing they will go. The elites will go a-hoaxing since they want to destroy and demonize their political opposition.

NO FEAR

The neo-Marxists and non-White racial activists will go a-hoaxing whenever they think it is to their advantage, because they know that the power structure will seldom call them on the carpet. Plus they can always count on their community's support no matter how outlandish their claims and demands are. And since the whole "equality" and multiracialism swindle is based on lies and fabrications to begin with, hoaxing of one kind or another is standard operating procedure for them.

And, of course, there are many whiners and losers and pathological anti-White misfits and attention-starved morons who are bright enough to figure out that one sure way to get sympathy and attention and even possibly celebrity and money is to become the latest victim of big, bad "White racism." They will certainly go a-hoaxing many, many times before the fall of the empire.

People such as myself, people who care about the future of our race, have virtually no influence in the halls of power in this country. We can't stop the hoaxers, and most of the time we can't expose them by ourselves either. All we have is a few honest police officers and reporters to do the exposing, and there are damned few of them around anymore. But thank God there are a few! In some cases, exposers of these hoaxes have been accused of "racism," and considering what such accusations can do to a career in the media or public service, it is a near miracle that any get exposed at all. Under such circumstances, it is reasonable to assume that there are many hoaxes as yet unexposed.

| "The current methodology employed by the FBI in compiling hate crime statistics is clearly inaccurate and misleading."

HATE CRIME STATISTICS ARE MISLEADING

Joseph E. Fallon

In the following viewpoint, Joseph E. Fallon argues that the statistics on hate crimes are inaccurate because the FBI—which is responsible for tracking hate crimes—does not use the same standards to identify victims and perpetrators of hate crimes. Several ethnic groups, such as Hispanics, are identified separately as victims of hate crimes, he asserts, but are classified with "whites" when they are the attackers. Therefore, he contends, the numbers of "white" perpetrators of hate crimes is exaggerated. For a truly accurate depiction of hate crimes, the FBI should use the same categories to identify perpetrators of hate crimes as it does for the victims, he maintains. Fallon researches ethnic and racial issues.

As you read, consider the following questions:
1. Who is considered Hispanic, according to U.S. public law?
2. What other two ethnic categories does Fallon recommend adopting to lessen the confusion over who should be considered "white"?
3. In the author's opinion, how should residents of the former Soviet republics in Asia be classified?

Reprinted, by permission, from Joseph E. Fallon, "The Politics of Hate Crimes Statistics," Chronicles: A Magazine of American Culture, May 1997 (vol. 21, no. 5).

The FBI's "Hate Crime Statistics"—preliminary figures for 1995 were released in November—are highly suspect because of the agency's flawed methodology. The problem is that, in recording and identifying the perpetrators of hate crimes, there are no strictly defined categories for thugs of "European-American," "Hispanic," or "Middle Eastern" descent. The term "Hispanic" has already been officially defined by Public Law 94-311 and Directive Number 15 of the Office of Management and Budget as "a person of Mexican, Puerto Rican, Cuban, Central or South American or other Spanish culture or origin, regardless of race." Employing the category "Middle Eastern" would probably be more convenient and less confusing than the heading currently used—"North Africa and Southwest Asia"—to identify anyone from that region of the world. And regarding the term "European-American," it has not been officially recognized by the federal government. It is essential that this last category be implemented and defined as "a person having origins in any of the original peoples of Europe—i.e., the British Isles, Iceland, and the European continent as bordered by the Pyrenees, the Caucasus, and the Ural mountains." This definition conforms to the standard already established by the federal government for defining Americans with origins in the Middle East and Asia, while avoiding the possibility of mistakenly including Hispanics in this category.

How Hate Crimes Are Determined

The FBI's current methodology for determining hate crimes is based on Public Law 101-275, the "Hate Crime Statistics Act" of 1990, which was enacted by Congress on April 23, 1990. This legislation mandated that the U.S. Attorney General establish guidelines and collect data "about crimes that manifest evidence of prejudice based on race, religion, sexual orientation, or ethnicity, including where appropriate the crimes of murder, non-negligent manslaughter; forcible rape; aggravated assault, simple assault, intimidation; arson; and destruction, damage, or vandalism of property." After the Attorney General delegated this responsibility to the director of the FBI, "the task of developing the procedures for, and managing the implementation of, the collection of hate crime data" was assigned to the Uniform Crime Reports Section of the FBI. Because of the time which elapsed before that FBI section received this assignment, 1991 was the first year for which hate crime statistics could be compiled. Since then, the specific types of hate crimes reported by the FBI have been: "Racial: anti-white, anti-black, anti-American Indian/Alaskan Native, anti-Asian/Pacific Islander, anti-multiracial group," "Ethnicity/National Origin: anti-Hispanic, anti-other ethnicity/national origin"; "Religious: anti-Jewish, anti-Catholic, anti-Protestant, anti-Islamic, anti-other religious group, anti-multireligious group, anti-atheism/agnosticism/etc."; "Sexual Orientation: anti-male homosexual, anti-female homosexual, anti-homosexual, anti-heterosexual, anti-bisexual."

DIFFERENT STANDARDS FOR VICTIMS AND PERPETRATORS

As the above listing makes clear, the FBI does identify victims of hate crimes by race, ethnicity/national origin, religion, or sexual orientation, in conformity with congressional intent. The FBI does not, however, apply the same standards to perpetrators of hate crimes. Instead, perpetrators are identified only by race: white, black, American Indian/Alaskan native, Asian/Pacific Islander, multiracial group, or unknown. The problem is that, according to this methodology, Hispanics are recognized as victims, but not as perpetrators. Since most Hispanics are often officially classified as "white"—the Department of Health and Human Services, for example, in its June 1996 report on illegitimacy rates in the United States for 1994, counted 91 percent of all unwed Hispanic women who gave birth as "white" in order to arrive at a 25 percent illegitimacy rate for "whites"—and since perpetrators of hate crimes are only recognized by race, Hispanics committing hate crimes are often classified as "white." The Department of Justice reports that for the federal prison system alone in 1991, the most recent year for which this statistic is available, Hispanics represented 28 percent of the total prison population, which then numbered 54,006. How many of these Hispanic convicts had committed hate crimes? Under the FBI's methodology, it is impossible to say.

Moreover, not only is it highly likely that a Hispanic's attack on an Asian, a black, or a Jew will be classified as a "white" hate crime, but apparently if one Hispanic attacks another Hispanic—for instance, if a Mexican attacks a Cuban—that too will be listed as a "white" hate crime. An additional problem, one making the Census Bureau's more restricted term of "White Not of Hispanic Origin" equally inappropriate, is that everyone from the Middle East, which is officially identified as North Africa and Southwest Asia (i.e., Arabs, Berbers, Baluchis, Kurds, Persians, Turks, etc.), is classified as "white." Any attacks or acts of intimidation or vandalism against Asians, blacks, or Jews by members of these communities would therefore also be classified as "white" hate crimes. Again, the FBI's methodology makes

A Different Racial-Crime Story

In mid-November of 1995, the FBI announced the results of its survey of "hate crime" in the United States. The Clinton FBI told the press that the largest category (58%) consisted of white crimes against blacks. This announcement represents an "imposed reality" by a highly politicized FBI made "sensitive" to leftist propaganda needs. That it is a case of political unreality is revealed by a comparison with the actual raw data from the Justice Department. Significantly, the real data has only been published in the foreign press. It has not been published in the United States because it shows a pattern which is exactly the opposite of that claimed by the FBI. Blacks attack whites at a much higher rate than do whites blacks. . . .

The "racist" facts which cannot be printed in the United States are very interesting. The raw FBI data tells a completely different racial-crime story than that announced to the press. The period during which blacks were called the highest victim category for "hate crimes," blacks actually killed whites 18 times more often than whites killed blacks. When comparing rates for all violent interracial crimes, blacks are over 50 times more likely to attack whites than whites are blacks. Further, the data suggests that much of this black-on-white crime may be racially motivated. . . . The explosion of black-on-white crime reflects politically generated hostilities of blacks towards whites and thus would constitute "hate crimes." The numbers are staggering. Nearly 25 million whites have suffered violent assault from blacks since 1964 and nearly 45,000 have been killed, a greater casualty figure than suffered during the Korean War. Journalist Paul Sheehan characterizes this phenomenon as a hidden war on whites. All this is going on in the background as the FBI announces that blacks are the highest victim category of their new "hate crimes" designation.

Lawrence Dawson, *American Information Newsletter*, July 1996.

---

it impossible to ascertain how many "white" hate crimes are really perpetrated by North Africans and Southwest Asians.

Members of these same communities, however, when they are the victims of hate crimes, are not classified as "white" but rather by their "ethnicity/national origin" or "religion." Therefore, according to the official records, North Africans and Southwest Asians, like Hispanics, can only be victims, not perpetrators, of hate crimes.

Who Is "White"?

For the five years for which hate crime statistics have been compiled, the FBI reports that the percentage of all hate crimes perpetrated by "whites" has been: 65 percent in 1991, 64 percent in 1992, 51 percent in 1993, 57 percent in 1994, and 59 percent in 1995. And because of its flawed methodology, the public is misled into believing that European-Americans are the principal perpetrators of the hate crimes against Hispanics, North Africans, and Southwest Asians. For people to assume that "white" is synonymous with "European-Americans" is understandable. After all, according to the 1990 Census, more than 93 percent of all "whites" *are* European-Americans. This fact does not mean, however, that over 93 percent of the "white-perpetrated hate crimes" are committed by European-Americans.

The meaninglessness of this "white" category can be seen in how the federal government treats the former Soviet Central Asian republics of Kazakhstan, Kirgyzstan, Tajikistan, Turkmenistan, and Uzbekistan. While the United Nations officially identifies these states as Asian—they are, after all, located in Asia and, with a few exceptions, are populated primarily by groups that are racially Asian—the U.S. Agency for International Development, the U.S. Census Bureau, and the U.S. Immigration and Naturalization Service all classify the five Central Asian republics as "European."

The current methodology employed by the FBI in compiling hate crime statistics is clearly inaccurate and misleading. If the FBI would employ the terms "European-American," "Hispanic," and "Middle Eastern" when identifying the perpetrators of such crimes, it could correct this problem and introduce some much-needed rationality to its operations. The true victims and perpetrators of these crimes could then be known and dealt with accordingly.

"All Americans deserve protection from hate."

THE DEFINITION OF HATE CRIMES SHOULD BE EXPANDED

Bill Clinton

Bill Clinton is the forty-second president of the United States. The following viewpoint is excerpted from a speech he gave at the White House Conference on Hate Crimes on November 10, 1997. Clinton argues that laws governing hate crimes should be expanded to include crimes against women, the disabled, and gays and lesbians, and that these laws should be strictly enforced. In addition to imposing laws, he asserts, society needs to teach children not to hate.

As you read, consider the following questions:

1. What steps is the Justice Department taking to reduce hate crimes, according to Clinton?
2. How will adding questions about hate crimes to the National Crime Victimization Survey help reduce hate crimes, in Clinton's opinion?
3. What are some of the methods that will be used to teach children not to hate, according to the author?

Reprinted from Bill Clinton's speech at the White House Conference on Hate Crimes, Washington D.C., November 10, 1997.

All over the world we see what happens when racial or ethnic or religious animosity joins with lawlessness. We've seen countries and people and families torn apart. We've seen countries go from peace to wholesale internecine slaughter in a matter of months. We've seen people rise up and fight each other over issues that they thought had been dormant for centuries.

TOO MANY STORIES OF HATE CRIMES

But even in America we hear too many stories like . . . the 13-year-old African American boy nearly beaten to death when he rode his bicycle through the wrong neighborhood, the gay American murdered as he walked home from work, the Asian American who lost her store to a firebomb hurled by a racist, the Jewish American whose house of worship was desecrated by swastikas.

We hear too many of these stories—stories of violent acts which are not just despicable acts of bias and bigotry, they are crimes. They strike at the heart of what it means to be an American. They are the antithesis of the values that define us as a nation. They have nothing to do with freedom or equality or respect for the law, and most importantly, they prevent us from respecting one another.

In 1996 I asked the American people to begin a great national conversation on race, to come together across all the lines that divide us into one America. We know we can only fight prejudice by fighting the misunderstanding and the ignorance and the fear that produce it. One of the things that I hope will come out of 1997 is a national affirmation that violence motivated by prejudice and hatred . . . hurts us all. Anybody who thinks that in the world of today and tomorrow, that he or she can hide from the kind of poison that we see in various places in our country, is living in a dream world. Whether we like it or not, our futures are bound together, and it is time we acted like it.

WHAT MUST BE DONE

The first thing we have to do is to make sure our nation's laws fully protect all of its citizens. Our laws already punish some crimes committed against people on the basis of race or religion or national origin, but we should do more. We should make our current laws tougher to include all hate crimes that cause physical harm. We must prohibit crimes committed because of a victim's sexual orientation, gender or disability. All Americans deserve protection from hate. . . .

The second thing we have to do is to make sure our civil

rights laws are consistently and vigorously enforced. Under Attorney General Janet Reno's leadership, the Justice Department has taken aim at hate crimes with more prosecutions and tougher punishments. Starting today, every United States Attorney [General] in our country will establish or expand working groups to develop enforcement strategies, share best practices, and educate the public about hate crimes. This national hate crimes network will marshal the resources of federal, state and local enforcement, community groups, educators, antiviolence advocates, to give us another powerful tool in the struggle against hate crimes.

GIVE THE FEDERAL GOVERNMENT THE POWER TO PROSECUTE HATE CRIMES

The Justice Department has jurisdiction over hate crimes based upon race, color, religion and national origin. The hate crime laws do not permit us to investigate or prosecute offenses motivated by a victim's disability, gender or sexual orientation. That is why the administration has urged Congress to enact the bipartisan hate crimes legislation. [No action has been taken as of August 1998.]

This bill is needed for two reasons. First, violent hate crimes based on sexual orientation, disability and gender are a serious problem not covered by current federal law. The federal government must have authority to prosecute those cases where state and local prosecutors are unable to.

Second, current federal law contains a problematic and often unnecessary hurdle for prosecutors that the victim must have been participating in one of several narrowly defined set of so-called "federal protected activities." This bill will do away with this unnecessary requirement to hate crime cases involving bodily injury that has hindered our efforts to prosecute violent purveyors of hate, and we must eliminate it.

Remarks by Bill Lann Lee at the Forum on Hate Crimes, February 18, 1998.

I'm also pleased to announce that we will assign over 50 more FBI agents and prosecutors to work on hate crimes enforcement. And the Justice Department will make its own hate crimes training curriculum available to state and local law enforcement training centers all around America.

Finally, the Department of Housing and Urban Development and the Justice Department are launching an important new initiative that will help victims of housing-related hate crimes bring action against their attackers and get money damages for the harm they suffer. . . .

Getting a True Count of Hate Crimes

Let me also say that in addition to enforcement, in addition to pushing for new laws, in addition to training our own people and others better, let's also admit one thing—we have a lot of law enforcement officials who have worked on this—a lot of hate crimes still go unreported. . . . If a crime is unreported, that gives people an excuse to ignore it.

I'm pleased to announce that today for the first time the National Crime Victimization Survey used by the Justice Department will finally include questions about hate crimes, so we can report them on a national basis along with others. It may seem like a small addition, but it will yield large results. It will give us a better measure of the number of hate crimes and it will increase what we know about how they occur.

Teaching Children Not to Hate

Let me say, lastly, all of us have to do more in our communities through organizations . . . and in our own homes and places of worship to teach all of our children about the dignity of every person. I'm very pleased that the Education and the Justice Departments will distribute to every school district in the country a hate crimes resource guide. The guide will direct educators to the materials they can use to teach tolerance and mutual respect. And also the Justice Department is launching a Web site where younger students can learn about prejudice and the harm it causes.

Children have to be taught to hate. And as they come more and more of age and they get into more and more environments where they can be taught that, we need to make sure that somebody is teaching them not to do so.

I wouldn't be surprised if, today, some of the skinheads that threw rocks and bottles at . . . a little girl have grown out of it and are frankly ashamed of what they did. I wouldn't be surprised if some of them weren't ashamed of it the day they did it—but they just wanted to go along, to get along, to be part of the group. . . .

So as important as it is to enforce the law, to punish people, to do all this—all this is very important. The most important thing we can do is to reach these kids while they're young enough to learn. Somebody is going to be trying to teach them to hate. We want to teach them a different way. And in the end, if we all do our part for that, we can make America one nation under God.

"If what one is thinking in the commission of a crime adds to the punishment, are we not on the threshold of making hate itself a crime?"

THE DEFINITION OF HATE CRIMES SHOULD NOT BE EXPANDED

Linda Bowles

In the following viewpoint, syndicated columnist Linda Bowles argues that the punishment for a crime should not be increased solely because of what the culprit was thinking at the time. Such an action will eventually lead to criminalizing hate, she contends. Furthermore, Bowles maintains, singling out some groups for special consideration as hate crime victims treats Americans unequally and is therefore unconstitutional.

As you read, consider the following questions:
1. What three factors must be considered when determining if a crime is a hate crime, according to Bowles?
2. In the author's opinion, what may be the underlying and undeclared motivation for hate crime legislation?
3. Why does the author believe that Bill Clinton's actions concerning hate crimes are inflammatory and selective?

Reprinted from Linda Bowles, "What Is a Hate Crime?" *Wanderer*, July 3, 1997, by permission of Linda Bowles and Creators Syndicate.

President Bill Clinton used one of his weekly radio addresses to attack hate crimes. He ordered the Justice Department to review the legislation on such crimes, and he called for a White House conference on the subject in November 1997.

Since left-wing, radical fundamentalists have already demonstrated their self-righteous readiness to shut up, shout down, and legally throttle anyone delivering messages they don't like, I thought I should have my say while it is still legal for me to do so.

What Is a Hate Crime?

What is a hate crime? It depends upon certain factors: the crime itself, who the victim is, and what the criminal is thinking and feeling at the time.

For example, if you burn down someone's house because you enjoy watching a good fire, you get a standard sentence. If, however, it can be proved that you burned down the house because it was owned by, shall we say, an Asian American and you hate Asian Americans, you get a more severe sentence—that is, unless you yourself are also an Asian American, in which case the arson is simply arson and not also a hate crime.

Let us beg a question: Is it a hate crime if the assailant smiles while lighting the fire, gives every evidence of having a good time doing it, and yells out for witnesses to hear, "I am not burning your house down because you are an Asian American but because I missed a two-foot putt yesterday and my eggs were overcooked this morning!"?

Problems with Legislating Against Hate Crimes

There are a number of problems associated with hate-crime legislation. If what one is thinking in the commission of a crime adds to the punishment, are we not on the threshold of making hate itself a crime? Are we drifting toward thought police and the legal codification of "politically correct," mostly liberal hatreds and prejudices?

One cannot help wondering why essentially everybody in America other than white, heterosexual males are entitled to protection by these kinds of laws. Why doesn't hate against white, heterosexual males count? Does this reflect a hateful attitude toward members of this group?

Indeed, is hatred of white, heterosexual males the underlying and undeclared motivation for hate-crime legislation?

If our purpose is to discourage hate-based crimes, why limit ourselves? There are many other groups who might qualify for hate-crime coverage by virtue of substantial public scorn and abuse.

How may we exclude such worthy contenders as flag burners, cigar aficionados, tobacco executives, postal workers, Communists, members of the militia, drunks, conservative columnists, lawyers, IRS agents, used-car salesmen, politicians, rednecks, and skinheads?

THE RELIGIOUS NEED PROTECTION

Why should these widely detested and frequently persecuted Americans be denied special protection against crimes of hate?

If any one group in the United States truly deserves special protection, it is the religious community. People who believe in God, trying to hang on to their values, are under attack from every direction. If they defend themselves, they are accused of bigotry and fanaticism.

In the spirit of our President's call to arms against crimes of hate, surely anyone who assaults, maligns, or harasses a proud and practicing Christian should get triple punishment, including enforced attendance at a brain-scrubbing sensitivity seminar designed by Jerry Falwell.

The President said, "It is time for us to mount an all-out assault on hate crimes." I say amen to that, although it is my personal opinion that this President's rhetoric about race and hate is often inflammatory and highly selective.

THE CRIMINALIZATION OF HATRED

Is hatred a moral crime against humanity? Of course it is. Is there any doubt that bigotry and hatred are at the root of incalculable human suffering, death, and injustice, and always have been? Of course not. . . .

Even if it were possible to determine the mindset in which a crime is committed, is it appropriate in a free society for the government to punish people for their inner motivations, feelings, and beliefs, however venomous those beliefs and feelings may be? Feelings and motivations, whether considered good or bad, are private and mercurial; laws are not. It doesn't take much imagination to foresee all manner of abuses of this approach. . . .

In a free society, the cure for hatred cannot be found through the police powers of the state to restrict its awful expressions. The cure lies in the minds of a free people who possess, without aid from government, the liberty to reject it.

Barbara Dority, *The Humanist*, May/June 1994.

When he ranted against "the epidemic of hate" involved in the burning of a number of black churches, why was he not outraged by the burning of a much larger number of white churches during the same time period?

The answer is obvious. The President is not about healing. He is about racial rabble-rousing.

I hereby call upon the President to set a good example by putting a stop to his own deceitful tactic of pitting Americans against each other for political gain.

As a shameful case in point, he has used the presidential pulpit to stereotype and scapegoat a special class of Americans.

AN UNCONSTITUTIONAL DIVISION OF AMERICA

Of course, I realize, as do many Americans, that Clinton is a socialist, but I do not think that excuses his call to class warfare and his incitement of envy and hate against those who are rich and successful.

This flagrantly unconstitutional business of dividing ourselves into groups and allocating treatments, advantages, and special rights based on what group we belong to has got to stop. It makes a mockery of what helped make America the shining light and envy of the world: the glorious idea that we are all Americans and all equal before the law.

"These [black church burnings] are not isolated, random incidents, but rather pieces in a pattern of hate crimes that have been underreported by the media and overlooked by law enforcement."

BLACK CHURCH BURNINGS ARE A SERIOUS HATE CRIMES PROBLEM

Melvin Talbert and Joan Brown Campbell

Melvin Talbert is a bishop and the president of the National Council of Churches (NCC), an organization of Protestant and Orthodox churches. Joan Brown Campbell is a minister and general secretary of the NCC. In the following viewpoint, which is taken from their written testimony at a hearing before the House Committee on the Judiciary, Talbert and Campbell contend that the burning of black churches in the southeastern United States is the result of a hate crime conspiracy by racist groups. Because many law enforcement officers do not take these church burnings seriously, the authors assert, the arsonists may feel emboldened to burn black churches during services.

As you read, consider the following questions:

1. How many black churches were burned between 1990 and 1996, according to the National Council of Churches?
2. What evidence do the authors present to support their contention that the church burnings are part of a racist conspiracy?
3. Who are the focus of many of the arson investigations, according to Talbert and Campbell?

Reprinted from the Congressional testimony of Melvin Talbert and Joan Brown Campbell, *Church Fires in the Southeast*, Hearing Before the Committee on the Judiciary, House of Representatives, 104th Cong., 2nd sess., May 21, 1996.

O n behalf of the National Council of the Churches of Christ in the U.S.A., we welcome this opportunity to testify on one of this country's most pressing social and moral crises—the epidemic of burnings, firebombings and other acts of racist violence directed at churches, most of them African-American churches, in several states of our nation.

The National Council of the Churches of Christ in the U.S.A.— often referred to as the National Council of Churches—is the pre-eminent expression in the United States of the movement for Christian unity. Its 33 Protestant and Orthodox member communions, to which 52 million people belong, work together with other church bodies to bring a wide sense of Christian community and to deepen the experience of unity. While we do not purport to speak for all members of the communions constituent to the National Council of Churches, we do speak for our policy-making body, the general assembly, whose 270 members are selected by those communions in numbers proportionate to their size. Founded in 1950 and headquartered in New York City, the National Council of Churches has spoken and acted consistently and forcefully for racial justice and civil rights, and against racism since its beginning.

INVESTIGATING THE ATTACKS

Currently the National Council of Churches is leading a major effort to investigate the attacks on black churches, provide practical and spiritual support to the victimized ministers and congregations, stop the attacks, bring the perpetrators to justice, make the general public aware of this wave of hate crimes and raise funds for rebuilding the churches, most of them underinsured and many not insured at all. Partners with us in this effort are the Center for Democratic Renewal, Atlanta, Ga. (formerly the National Anti-Klan Network), which has been monitoring white supremacist movements since 1979 and which since late 1995 systematically has been investigating the racist attacks on churches; and the Center for Constitutional Rights, New York City, which successfully has brought civil suits against the Ku Klux Klan and is preparing to bring legal action against perpetrators of the church attacks.

Since March 5, 1996, NCC teams have visited destroyed and damaged churches in Tennessee, Alabama, Mississippi, Georgia and Louisiana, and we are planning visits to South Carolina, Arkansas, Georgia and other states. On all these visits we go to the sites of churches that have been destroyed or damaged, and gather firsthand testimony from pastors, deacons and other members of these churches.

Our coalition's research has documented that, as of May 21, 1996, 57 black and interracial churches have been bombed, burned or vandalized in Alabama, Georgia, Tennessee, Arkansas, Mississippi, South Carolina, Louisiana and other states since January 1990. Twenty-five of these violent acts have occurred in 1996 alone. Among the most recent attacks was that which destroyed a black church in Tennessee on May 14, 1996, the very same day that an NCC delegation was visiting Nashville to speak with pastors whose churches had been burned.

We submit that these manifestations of domestic terrorism demand the highest degree of bipartisan attention at the federal, state and local levels. This is not a Democratic or Republican issue, but rather an American problem that should arouse moral outrage and condemnation from all people irrespective of their race, ethnic origin, religious affiliation or political orientation. Furthermore, we call for strong statements of resolve from both the administration and the Congress that this and all forms of racist violence will not be permitted to continue, and that the perpetrators will be sought out aggressively and brought to justice.

STRIKING SIMILARITIES

Our investigations have uncovered striking similarities in these incidents, parallels that constitute a pattern of abuses—including the use of Molotov cocktails and other incendiary devices, the spray-painting of racist graffiti, the targeting of churches with a history of strong advocacy for African-American rights, and racist notes and letters left in the mailboxes of pastors. Many churches were attacked on or around Jan. 15, Martin Luther King Jr. Day (five of those in 1996 and five in 1995).

The 30 persons so far arrested and/or convicted for these crimes are all white males between the ages of 15 and 45, with several of them admitting to be members of such racist groups as the Aryan Faction, Skinheads for White Justice and the Ku Klux Klan. We suspect, however, that many more perpetrators of these crimes have not been arrested and brought to justice because investigations to date have focused in large measure on the pastors and members of the burned churches rather than on the violent history of the above-mentioned racist groups.

Indeed, many law enforcement authorities at the local, state and federal levels continue to deny any connections among the several firebombings and say they doubt a conspiracy or motivation based on racism. Moreover, many local officials have told victims that theirs are isolated cases, the results of accidents or electrical fires.

The NCC has been provided with testimony from some of the affected pastors that racial epithets scrawled onto the remaining facades of their churches were immediately painted over by law enforcement officials without the consent of the church.

A Depraved Act

It's hard to think of a more depraved act of violence than the destruction of a place of worship. . . .

Every family has a right to expect that when they walk into a church or synagogue or mosque each week they will find a house of worship, not the charred remnants of a hateful act done by cowards in the night. We must rise up as a national community to safeguard the right of every citizen to worship in safety. That is what America stands for.

Bill Clinton radio address, June 8, 1996.

In addition to several churches in Tennessee, private homes and a lodge in Clarksville were firebombed and shotgunned. It was in the hills of Tennessee where the "whites-only" "Good Ole Boys Round-Up" meetings took place in 1995 and among the participants were known agents of the Treasury Department's Alcohol, Tobacco and Firearms (ATF) Division, one of the federal agencies investigating the church bombings.

Dissatisfaction over the Investigations

One of the most disturbing findings from the NCC's tour of Mississippi, Tennessee and Louisiana communities where black church burnings had occurred was a consensus of dissatisfaction and discontent expressed by the pastors and the congregations over the manner of the investigations conducted by state and federal authorities. We encountered a unanimous dismay that the investigations are concentrating on pastors and parishioners, implying that they set their own churches on fire.

Subtle implications are made that it was for the insurance money, even though most churches are uninsured or underinsured. Some of the pastors have been asked to take polygraph tests. Church records have been demanded, and church members interrogated to the point of tears. Credible leads provided by the pastors have not been followed up by the investigators and, to date, none of the victimized churches has been informed of the results or of the progress of the investigations. Without exception, the victims of these hate crimes said they felt intimidated by the very forces they had hoped would provide them with protection and would alleviate their anxieties. They fear that if these crimes go unnoticed and unpunished the perpetrators may become so emboldened as to attempt future firebombings during an actual church service with worshipers in attendance.

Although many of the pastors and other church leaders have received death threats, there have been no investigations of these threatening calls, and no protection has been offered to the clergy. Furthermore, there is evidence that the 57 incidents we have documented to date are only a small indication of the number of attacks actually taking place around the country.

It is our contention that these are not isolated, random incidents, but rather pieces in a pattern of hate crimes that have been underreported by the media and overlooked by law enforcement. It is a sad state of affairs that this nation is quietly and, in many cases, unwittingly accepting the racist destruction of houses of worship. The frightening fact is that white hate groups are growing faster than at any time in recent history, yet most of the country remains in a state of denial that such racism and bigotry is widespread.

A CAMPAIGN TO END THE HATE CRIMES

The National Council of Churches is determined to proceed with its campaign to put an end to these crimes of racial hatred, to restore the houses of worship that have been destroyed or damaged and to demand that thorough, impartial, nonintimidating investigations be carried out by the Federal Bureau of Investigation and the ATF.

| "There is no compelling evidence of any organized racist conspiracy to burn African-American Churches."

BLACK CHURCH BURNINGS ARE NOT A SERIOUS HATE CRIMES PROBLEM

Mindszenty Report

During the spring and summer of 1996, the media reported that a racist conspiracy was responsible for the burning of African-American churches in the southeast. Those reports are false and misleading, according to the editors of the Mindszenty Report. They argue that children, known arsonists, lightning, insurance defrauders, and teenagers high on drugs or alcohol are responsible for starting many of the fires that burned the churches. Those who claim that racists are responsible for the church burnings are not soothing racial tensions, but rather inflaming them, the editors contend. The Mindszenty Report is a monthly publication of conservative Catholic social and political commentary.

As you read, consider the following questions:

1. How many African-American churches were targets of suspected arson during the first six months of 1996, as cited by the authors?
2. Of the churches investigated as potential targets of arson, how many were positively cleared of being the target of racist arsonists, according to the authors?
3. According to Michael Fumento, who is responsible for the rumors of a racist conspiracy?

Reprinted, by permission of the Cardinal Mindszenty Foundation, from "Burning Churches: Racism or Race-Baiting?" Mindszenty Report, August 1996.

On January 20, 1996, the *New York Times* alerted the media and nation that the U.S. Treasury Department's BATF (Bureau of Alcohol, Tobacco & Firearms) was investigating a rash of arsons and suspicious fires at 25 churches across the nation where congregations were predominantly African-American.

Of particular note at the time was a January 8, 1996, fire that had gutted a church in Knoxville, Tennessee, whose assistant pastor was Reggie White, the legendary Green Bay Packers defensive lineman football hero. Before its torching, the integrated church had been spray-painted with racist graffiti.

While the private National Fire Protection Association—the only source that keeps records on such traumatic calamities— reports church burnings declined to 520 in 1994 from 1,420 in 1980, and *USA Today* notes (7/1/96) "white churches are burning at a similar pace" as African-American churches—that's not what headlines were reporting.

From the 25 suspicious arsons noted by the *Times* on Jan. 20, by the end of June 1996 the total of African-American churches burned had reached 65. Various national fundraising organizations were placing full-page ads in the *Times* (6/14/96 and 7/17/96) to warn about a resurgence of racism in the U.S. (which only contributions to their treasuries could help stifle.)

Not only that, for six months following the first *Times* story on African-American church burnings, there [were] special Congressional hearings, over 2,000 articles in newspapers according to a database media search, talk radio and network news features, a "hearing" by the Congressional "Black Caucus," presidential visits to burnt churches, a new federal law outlawing church burnings, and a joint federal task force consisting of some 250 BATF and FBI agents directed to investigate every suspected African-American church arson no matter how little damage.

While the *Wall Street Journal*, on June 12, 1996, pointed out that President Bill Clinton "by expressing sympathy for the victims and pushing for stronger federal action, can strengthen his support among minority voters without fearing a backlash from white voters," all Americans should be enraged about the criminal burning of *any* church. Not only is the image of a burning church or cross a symbol of racial hatred, it is also an attack on Christianity, the First Amendment of the U.S. Constitution and individual property rights.

Racism Is Not the Reason

In the summer of 1964, following the bombing of the Sixteenth Street Baptist Church in Birmingham, Alabama, in which four little girls—Denise McNair, Cynthia Wesley, Carole Robertson and Mae Collins—lost their lives, 34 African-American churches in the South were burned over a 3-month period. Some would have us believe—thirty years later, after great strides have been made toward racial harmony and justice—that today's African-American church burnings are a return to the troubled past. That is not true.

Of the 65 African-American churches cited in media reports as being targets of possible racist arson from January to the end of June 1996, many are still under investigation. In at least 25 of those cases, however, racism probably had nothing to do with it.

WHO REALLY SET THE FIRES

The *Mindszenty Report* has researched current available information, local press clippings and other sources on the 65 church burnings and found:

• One of the 65 listed church burnings was actually $50 worth of damage to a storeroom set by children in day care playing with matches. Another burning was the result of a 9-year-old African-American boy setting fire to a storage shed which quickly spread to a nearby chapel. Three black children aged 7 to 12 were arrested and released, with no charges filed, for setting a carpet afire in a South Carolina church—another of the 65 listed church burnings. Still another of the 65 was nothing more than $90 worth of damage to a trash can burned in the vicinity of a church in North Carolina.

• Known firebugs were arrested in at least three of the 65 burnings—all of them young black men or teens. A 26-year-old white man with a history of pyromania was arrested for burning a church in Texas and eight other buildings in the same vicinity. In Mississippi, another white man described as "a life-long firebug with the mind of a child" started fires in several buildings near a church which winds whipped to the church's tar-paper roof. Firefighters quickly extinguished flames with no damage. The church's black pastor said the incident was "not even worth talking about"—yet it is included in the list of 65 burned churches. A cigarette dropped near the entrance of one of the 65 burned churches, by a heavy-smoking deacon, is the suspected cause of a fire that destroyed a church in Lauderdale, Mississippi.

• At New Liberty Baptist in Tyler, Alabama, a 19-year-old white volunteer fireman admitted setting one of the 65 fires to impress his superiors with his firefighting skills. Another of the 65 was actually an old union hall being renovated in Shreveport,

Louisiana, by a congregation consisting of 11 adults and 30 children.

• The pastor of one of the 65 burned churches says he saw a bolt of lightning strike during a thunderstorm and is sure that was the cause. Insurance investigators determined an accidental fire around the vicinity of an air-conditioner unit at Longridge CME Methodist in Waskom, Texas, was the cause and paid full coverage to help rebuild.

• On the other hand, insurance fraud is suspected in several of the 65 church burnings. In one, a black contractor who may have been running out of money is under investigation for setting fire to a fellowship hall as a financial cover-up. In another of the 65 fires—which occurred in a locked church where every window had been sealed and barred and the congregation was attending services elsewhere—the local minister resigned and moved away after collecting insurance.

• In one case that has stirred some media attention, the pastor of one of the 65 churches who met with President Clinton and testified before the House Judiciary Committee on the issue of church burnings, has also been tied to five other fires, including ones that destroyed his home and a business. Although he collected large insurance payoffs, he vehemently denies any collusion in the incidents.

SATANISM AND SUBSTANCE ABUSE

Illegal drug use, alcohol abuse and Satanism—not racism—played major roles in the burning of a number of the 65 churches. Here are some *Mindszenty Report* findings:

• At Butler Chapel AME in Orangeburg, S.C., one black and two white teenage boys broke into the church to hold a Satanic rite. In a scuffle, a candle was knocked over and set the church afire. Pastor Patrick Mellerson, who was one of a group of ministers who met recently with President Clinton, notes: "This country has no morals anymore."

• In rural Tennessee near Knoxville, Michael Jett and two cousins consumed six cases of beer mixed with Valium before setting off to find Jett's daughter who had run off to Knoxville with a black man. After a night in the city, meeting only prostitutes and pimps, the three tossed Molotov cocktails into Friendship Baptist in Columbia, Tennessee, and Canaan AME at Mt. Pleasant. All are now serving three years in prison and must pay the churches $20,000 in damages. White neighbors in Columbia turned out in full force to condemn the church burning and to help in rebuilding so that the African-American church's congregation missed not a single Sunday service.

• St. John Baptist in Dixiana, S.C., is one of the nation's oldest African-American congregations, dating back to the American Revolution. In the past ten years over 300 arrests for vandalism have been made there by local police. An afternight hang-out for teens, in two recent incidents someone tried to exhume a grave and, after a Satanic Black Mass, riddled pews with shotgun fire, smashed an organ with an ax and defecated on the church's altar cloths.

• After a day of drinking beer and smoking pot, three white teenagers torched two African-American churches near Summit, Mississippi. All are now serving jail terms.

Reprinted by permission of Chuck Asay and Creators Syndicate.

• One Hispanic and two white teens, parked behind a church in Greenville, Texas, smoking crack cocaine, were arrested for the flaming of the New Light House of Prayer and Church of the Living God, two of the 65 media-designated burned churches. They were released after a member of one of the African-American churches identified a youth she saw speeding away from the fire scene with three other accomplices. Mark Anthony Young, an 18-year-old black teen, has admitted setting fire to the two churches and is suspected in more than 20 other arsons in the North Texas area.

• Sentenced to 3-years probation, 18-year-old Donnie Hurst

spent all day drinking liquor before entering Faith Whole Truth Holiness Church in Pennington, Alabama, setting fire to an American Flag, and then the rest of the small African-American chapel.

• Also serving prison time is John Jason Bakenhaus, leader of a media-described white supremist group called *Aryan Faction*. Bakenhaus, 21, and Charles Neblett, 18, were found guilty of burning down Benevolent Lodge No. 12 in Adams, Tennessee, a meeting hall used by African-American Baptists for services. A loner with no friends, Bakenhaus says he began smoking pot at age 12 and tried every other drug he could get his hands on, including LSD, as a teen. His "white supremist group" included a handful of similarly-inclined middle-school and slightly older outcast youths around Clarksville, Tennessee.

• A mentally-disturbed 13-year-old white girl, claiming to be a Satanist, was the perpetrator of the most highly-publicized of all 65 recent church burnings. Her target—the Matthews Murland Presbyterian in Charlotte, N.C.—appeared ablaze on the front page of the June 8 *New York Times* headlined "Another Fire at a Southern Black Church" and, soon thereafter, in full-page newspaper ads denouncing this as an example of a resurgence of racism in the U.S. To the contrary, the girl told authorities she didn't know it was an African-American church; she burned the 93-year-old wooden chapel because it bore a cross, a symbol of Christianity.

A Race-Baiting Issue

Rather than racism, the burning churches problem appears to be a race-baiting issue instead. When President Clinton told his weekly radio show listeners he had "vivid and painful memories of black churches being burned in my own state when I was a child," his own pro-Clinton Arkansas *Democratic-Gazette* newspaper conducted an exhaustive check of state civil rights leaders and none could remember *a single such church burning*. When Vice President Al Gore, speaking to the press after a meeting with governors from states affected by recent church burnings declared "the conspiracy is racism itself," the liberal *New Yorker* magazine (July 15, 1996) noted "the conspiracy is racism itself" phrase was used earlier that day by a Left-Wing public interest group called *Center for Democratic Renewal* which had pushed the church burning issue to national attention.

The *New Yorker*, in fact, points out that the truth about recent church burnings is less apocalyptic than what the public has been led to believe—in reality a myth that does "disservice to history" in pretending "Martin Luther King accomplished nothing."

Likewise, the liberal *Washington Post* columnist Edwin Yoder admits "treating the church fires as morally clearer than the facts warrant, suits political as well as journalistic convenience" and concludes "the initial clamor over this vile expression on 'racism' is not sustained by closer analysis." His *Post* colleague, African-American syndicated columnist William Raspberry, says Yoder, "asked himself recently what his reaction might be if 'the arsonous campaign against black churches turns out to be no such thing' (and replied) 'Will I be profoundly relieved? Or will I be just a little disappointed? I'm not proud of it, but the answer, I fear is: Both.'"

Yet another eminent journalistic voice of liberalism, the *New Republic* magazine (July 15 & 22, 1996, issues) was "disturbed by rampant political posturing" surrounding the church burnings. To wit:

"The reactions to the wave of Southern church burnings have followed a familiar pattern: first the speaker calmly denies there's any evidence of a conspiracy, then feverishly paints an image of conspiracy. Take Congressman John Conyers, who began a May 21, 1996, hearing on the subject tentatively: 'It's also unclear how many were racially motivated.' By the end, the word 'fire' had mutated into 'firebombed,' the uncertain conclusions had turned into the 'worst form of domestic terrorism.' Two weeks later, a Conyers's press release invoked the KKK, cross burnings and lynchings. . . ."

NO EVIDENCE OF A CONSPIRACY

There is no compelling evidence of any organized racist conspiracy to burn African-American churches. *So where did the campaign to suggest there IS one originate?* Along with the *New Yorker*, former U.S. Commission on Civil Rights attorney Michael Fumento singles out one "activist group (that) has taken the media and the nation on a wild ride." Following are quotes from Fumento's revealing July 8, 1996, *Wall Street Journal* story on the details:

"It turns out the main source is the *Center for Democratic Renewal* (CDR), a group whose mission, says its promotional literature, is to work 'with progressive activists and organizations to build a movement to counter right-wing rhetoric and public policy initiatives.'

"Originally called the National Anti-Klan Network, it changed its name when the Klan largely fell apart in the 1980's. But instead of seeing that as a sign of declining bigotry, the CDR has continued for more than a decade to issue statements and reports 'discovering' a sudden resurgence in racist activity.

"The CDR's agenda goes well beyond rooting out genuine bigotry; the group tars mainstream conservatives with the same brush as racist criminals. 'There's only a slippery slope between conservative religious persons and those that are really doing the burning,' the Rev. C. T. Vivian, the CDR's chairman said." (Editor's Note: David J. Garrow in his sympathetic book on the late civil rights leader, *The FBI and Martin Luther King, Jr.* [Norton, 1981] says as far back as the 1940's, a Rev. C.T. Vivian was named a Communist Party member from Illinois.)

"In late March," continues Michael Fumento's *Wall Street Journal* account, "the CDR held a press conference and released a preliminary report showing a tremendous surge in arsons against black churches beginning in 1990. 'You're talking about a well-organized white-supremist movement,' Rev. Mac Charles Jones, a CDR board member, told the *Christian Science Monitor*. On CNN he referred to 'domestic terrorism.' From there the story snowballed."

The Ultimate Irony

Quoting Alabama's State Fire Marshall John Robison on black church burnings: "There have been no dramatic increases, except for this year because of the media hype," Fumento notes that other states' officials have said the same thing.

"Here lies the ultimate irony," Fumento concludes, "by claiming there has been an epidemic of black church burnings, it appears that the CDR and the media may have actually sparked one. They have also fomented tremendous racial division and caused great fear among Southern black church-goers. What the Ku Klux Klan can no longer do, a group established to fight the Klan is doing instead."

"Nothing in the Constitution . . .
*requires that hate speech receive
protection*."

HATE SPEECH IS A SERIOUS HATE CRIMES PROBLEM

Richard Delgado and Jean Stefancic

Hate speech is speech that denigrates a person or a group of people. Free speech proponents argue that hate speech must be permitted in order to ensure that the right to engage in other forms of speech is not compromised. In the following viewpoint, Richard Delgado and Jean Stefancic reject this argument. Several countries have banned hate speech with no damage to the right of free speech, they assert. Furthermore, Delgado and Stefancic argue, when hate speech is permitted under the guise of protecting all speech, the only result is a systemic harm to its victims. Hate speech is permitted, the authors maintain, because it is used by those in power to keep women and minorities in subordinate positions. Richard Delgado is the Charles Inglis Thomson Professor of Law at the University of Colorado. Jean Stefancic is a documents librarian and research associate at the University of Colorado School of Law. They are the authors of *Must We Defend Nazis?* from which this viewpoint is taken.

As you read, consider the following questions:

1. On what basis do free speech proponents justify protecting the rights of Nazis, according to the authors?
2. What examples do the authors present to support their contention that the United States has not protected free speech in the past?
3. According to Delgado and Stefancic, how does permitting hate speech influence society's attitudes toward minorities?

Reprinted, by permission, from Richard Delgado and Jean Stefancic, *Must We Defend Nazis?* (New York: New York University Press, 1997).

The argument that we must protect the speech we hate in order to protect that which we hold dear is a special favorite of certain commentators who advocate an unfettered First Amendment. For example, Samuel Walker, the author of a history of the American Civil Liberties Union (ACLU) and another of the hate-speech controversy, writes that the ACLU believes that "every view, no matter how ignorant or harmful we may regard it, has a legal and moral right to be heard." He explains that banning ignorant and hateful propaganda against Jews, for instance, "could easily lead to the suppression of other ideas now regarded as moderate and legitimate." The free speech victories that have been won in defending Nazi and other unpopular speech, Walker points out, have also been used to protect pro–civil rights messages. In two books and a series of law review articles, Nadine Strossen, the president of the ACLU, echoes Walker's views. "If the freedom of speech is weakened for one person, group, or message," according to Strossen, we will soon have no free speech right left at all. Thus, for example, "the effort to defend freedom for those who choose to create, pose for, or view pornography is not only freedom for this particular type of expression but also freedom of expression in general." In *Speaking of Race, Speaking of Sex: Hate Speech, Civil Rights, and Civil Liberties*, Anthony Griffin and Henry Louis Gates advance positions similar to Strossen's. Gates writes that when the ACLU defended the right of neo-Nazis to march in Skokie, a predominantly Jewish suburb of Chicago where a number of Holocaust survivors lived, it did so to protect and fortify the constitutional right of free speech. If free speech can be tested and upheld to protect even Nazi speech, "then the precedent will make it that much stronger in all the less obnoxious cases." Griffin, who forfeited his position with the Texas National Association for the Advancement of Colored People (NAACP) in order to defend a Klan organization, reiterates the ACLU position through a series of three fables, all of which reinforce the notion that the only way to have a strong, vibrant First Amendment is to protect Nazi speech, racist speech, and so on. Otherwise, the periphery will collapse and the government will increasingly regulate speech we regard as central to our system of politics and government.

OTHER VIEWS

This type of argument is not just the favorite of the ACLU and its friends. Respected constitutional commentators have employed similar reasoning. Lee Bollinger, for instance, posits that Nazi speech should be protected not because people should value their message in the slightest or believe it should be seriously entertained, but because protection of such speech reinforces our society's commitment to tolerance. Laurence Tribe advances a variant of the same theme. In explaining that there is no principled basis for regulating speech based on content or viewpoint, Tribe states, "If the Constitution forces government to allow people to march, speak, and write in favor or preach brotherhood, and justice, then it must also require government to allow them to advocate hatred, racism, and even genocide." As put forward by these and other commentators, then, the "speech we hate" argument takes on a small number of variants. Some argue that there must be a wall around the periphery to protect speech that we hold dear. Others reason that speech that lies at the periphery must be protected if we are to strengthen impulses or principles, such as toleration, that are important to society. . . .

As we mentioned, the extreme-case argument is rarely if ever defended or justified. Rather, its supporters put it forward as an article of faith, without reason or support, as though it were self-evidently true. But is it?

LACK OF EMPIRICAL SUPPORT

If protecting hate speech and pornography were essential to safeguarding freedom of inquiry and a flourishing democratic politics, we would expect to find that nations that have adopted hate-speech rules and curbs against pornography would suffer a sharp erosion of the spirit of free inquiry. But this has not happened. A host of Western industrialized nations, including Sweden, Italy, Canada, and Great Britain, have instituted laws against hate speech and hate propaganda, many in order to comply with international treaties and conventions requiring such action. Many of these countries have traditions of respect for free speech at least the equal of ours. No such nation has reported any erosion of the atmosphere of free speech or debate. At the same time, the United States, which until recently has refused to put such rules into effect, has a less than perfect record of protecting even political speech. We persecuted communists, hounded Hollywood writers out of the country, and harassed and badgered such civil rights leaders as Josephine Baker, Paul Robeson, and W.E.B. DuBois in a campaign of personal and professional smears that ruined their reputations and denied them the ability to make a living. In recent times, conservatives inside and outside the Administration have disparaged progressives to the point where many are now afraid to use the "liberal" word to describe themselves. Controversial artists are denied federal funding. Museum exhibits that depict the A-bombing of Hiroshima have been ordered modified. If political speech lies at the center of the First Amendment, its protection seems to be largely independent of what is taking place at the periphery. There may, indeed, be an inverse correlation. Those institutions most concerned with social fairness have proved to be the ones most likely to promulgate anti-hate-speech rules. Part of the reason seems to be recognition that hate speech can easily silence and demoralize its victims, discouraging them from participating in the life of the institution. If so, enacting hate-speech rules may be evidence of a commitment to democratic dialogue, rather than the opposite, as some of their opponents maintain.

A PARADOXICAL METAPHOR

A second reason why we ought to distrust the core-periphery argument is that it rests on a paradoxical metaphor that its proponents rarely if ever explain or justify. Suppose, for example, that one were in the business of supplying electricity to a region. One has competitors—private utility companies, suppliers of gas heaters, and so on. Ninety-nine percent of one's business consists of supplying electricity to homes and businesses, but one also supplies a small amount of electricity to teenagers to recharge the batteries of their Walkmans. It would surely be a strange business decision to focus all or much of one's advertising campaign on the much smaller account. Or take a more legal example. Protecting human security is surely a core value for the police. Yet, it would be a peculiar distribution of police services if a police chief were to reason: human life is the core value which we aim to protect; therefore, we will devote the largest proportion of our resources toward apprehending shoplifters and loiterers.

There are situations in which the core-periphery argument does make sense. Providing military defense of a territory may be one; ecology, where protecting lizards may be necessary in order to protect hawks, may be another. But ordinarily the suggestion that to protect a value or thing at its most extreme reaches is necessary in order to protect it at its core requires, at the very least, an explanation. Defenders of hate speech who deploy this argument have not provided one. And, in the meantime, a specious argument does great harm. It treats in grand, exalted terms the harm of suppressing racist speech, drawing illegitimate support from the broad social justification—social dialogue among citizens. The harm to hate speech's victims, out on the periphery, by contrast is treated atomistically, as though it were an isolated event, a mere one-time-only affront to feelings. An injury characterized in act-utilitarian terms obviously cannot trump one couched in broad rule-utilitarian terms. The Nazi derives a halo effect from other, quite legitimate and valuable cases of speech, while the black is seen as a lone, quirky grievant with hypersensitive feelings. But, in reality, hate speech is part of a concerted set of headwinds, including many other cases of such speech, that this particular African American victim will experience over the course of his or her life. If we are willing to defend speech in broad social terms, we should be able to consider systemic, concerted harms as well.

The speech-we-hate argument draws plausibility only by ignoring this symmetry. It draws on a social good to justify an evil deemed only individual, but which in fact is concerted and societywide. The unfairness of collapsing the periphery and the center as absolutists do would be made dear if we rendered the argument: "We protect the speech they hate in order to protect that which we love." But not only is the argument unfair in this sense, it ignores what makes hate speech peripheral *as speech* in the first place. Face to face hate speech—slurs, insults, put-downs, and epithets—are not referential. The recipient learns nothing new about himself or herself. Rather, they are more like performatives, relocating the speaker and victim in social reality. Hate speech is not about the real, but the hyperreal. . . .

FIRST AMENDMENT ROMANTICISM

With hate speech and pornography, heeding the ACLU's totalist argument introduces special dangers of its own. Hate speech lies at the periphery of the First Amendment, as the proponents of the argument quickly concede. Yet the reason why hate speech does so is that it implicates the interest of another group, minorities, in not being defamed, reviled, stereotyped, insulted, badgered, and harassed. Permitting a society to portray a relatively powerless group in this fashion helps construct a stigma-picture or stereotype according to which its members are lascivious, lazy, carefree, immoral, stupid, and so on. This stereotype guides action, making life much more difficult for minorities in transactions that clearly matter: getting a job, renting an apartment, hailing a cab. But it also diminishes the credibility of minority speakers, inhibiting their ability to have their points of view taken seriously, in politics or anywhere else—surely a result that is at odds with the First Amendment and the marketplace of ideas. This is an inevitable result of treating peripheral regions of a value as entitled to the same weight we afford that

TALKING BACK AS A MEANS OF COMBATING HATE SPEECH

Those who hurl racial epithets do so because they feel empowered to utter them. One who talks back is seen as issuing a direct challenge to that power. Many racist remarks are delivered by a crowd to an individual, a situation in which responding in kind would be foolhardy. Many highly publicized cases of racial assault began in just this fashion: a group began badgering a black person; the victim talked back, and paid with his or her life. Other racist remarks are delivered in a cowardly fashion, by means of graffiti scrawled on a campus wall late at night or a leaflet placed under a student's dormitory door. In these situations, talking back, of course, is impossible.

Richard Delgado and David Yun, "Pressure Valves and Bloodied Chickens," in *The Price We Pay*, Laura J. Lederer and Richard Delgado, eds., 1995.

---

value when it is centrally implicated: we convey the impression that those other values—the ones responsible for the continuum in the first place—are of little worth. And when those other values are central to the social construction of a human being or social group, the dangers of undervaluing their interests rise sharply. Their interests are submerged today—in the valuing a court or decision-maker is asked to perform. And they are submerged in the future, because their owners are thereafter the bearers of a stigma, one which means they need not be taken fully into account in future deliberations. Permitting one social group to speak disrespectfully of another habituates and encourages speakers to continue speaking that way in the future. This way of speaking becomes normalized, inscribed in hundreds of plots, narratives, and scripts; it becomes part of culture, what everyone knows. The reader may wish to reflect on changes he or she has surely observed since the early 1980s. During the civil rights era of the sixties and early seventies, African Americans and other minorities were spoken of respectfully. Then, beginning in the late seventies and eighties, racism was spoken in code. Today, however, op-ed columns, letters to the editor, and political speeches deride and blame them outspokenly. Anti-minority sentiment need no longer be spoken in code but is right out in the open. We have changed our social construct of the black from unfortunate victim and brave warrior to welfare leeches, unwed mothers, criminals, and untalented low-IQ affirmative action beneficiaries who take away jobs from more talented and deserving whites. The slur, sneer, ethnic joke, and most especially face-to-face hate speech are the main vehicles that have made this change possible.

WHY THE CORE-PERIPHERY ARGUMENT PERSISTS

As we have seen, the extreme case (or core-periphery) argument rests on an unexamined, paradoxical metaphor. . . . What accounts for this argument's rhetorical attraction and staying power? We believe the principal reason is that hate speech and pornography today do not lie at the periphery of the First Amendment, as the ACLU and other advocates urge, but at its center. In former times, society was much more structured than it is now. Citizens knew their places. Women and blacks understood they were not the equals of white men—the Constitution formally excluded them, and coercive social and legal power reminded them of that if they were ever tempted to step out of line. It was not necessary constantly to reinforce this—an occasional reminder would do. Today, however, the formal mechanisms that maintained status and caste are gone or repealed. All that is left is speech and the social construction of reality. Hate speech has replaced formal slavery, Jim Crow laws, female subjugation, and Japanese internment as means to keep subordinate groups in line. In former times, political speech was indeed the center of the First Amendment. Citizens (white, property-owning males, at any rate) did take a lively interest in politics. They spoke, debated, wrote tracts, corresponded with each other about how the Republic ought to be governed. They did not much speak about whether women were men's equals, should be allowed to hold jobs or vote, whether blacks were the equals of whites, because this was not necessary—the very ideas were practically unthinkable.

MAINTAINING THE STATUS QUO

Today, the situation is reversed. Few Americans vote, or can even name their representative in Washington. Politics has deteriorated to a once-every-four-years ritual of attack ads, catch phrases, sound bites, and image manicuring. At the same time, however, politics in the sense of jockeying for social position has greatly increased in intensity and virulence. Males are anxious and fearful of advances by women; whites fear crime and vengeful behavior from blacks; and so on. Hate speech today is a central weapon in the struggle by the empowered to maintain their position in the face of formerly subjugated groups clamoring for change. It is a means of disparaging the opposition while depicting one's own resistance to sharing opportunities as principled and just. Formerly, the First Amendment and free speech were used to make small adjustments within a relatively peaceful political order consisting of propertied white males.

Now it is used to postpone macroadjustments and power-sharing between that group and others: it is, in short, an instrument of majoritarian identity politics. Nothing in the Constitution . . . requires that hate speech receive protection. But ruling elites are unlikely to relinquish it easily, since it is an effective means of postponing social change.

In the sixties, it was possible to believe [the] optimistic hypothesis that gains for blacks stemming from the gallant struggle for civil rights would end up benefiting all of society. It was true for a time, at least, that the hard-won gains by a decade of civil rights struggle did broaden speech, due process, and assembly rights for whites as well as blacks. Today, however, there has been a stunning reversal. Now, the reciprocal injury—inhibition of the right to injure others—has been elevated to a central place in First Amendment jurisprudence. The injury—of being muffled when one would otherwise wish to disparage, terrorize, or burn a cross on a black family's lawn—is now depicted as a prime constitutional value. The interest convergence between black interests and broadened rights for whites lasted but a short time. Now, the ACLU defends Aryan supremacists, while maintaining that this is best for minorities, too. Blanket resistance to hate-speech regulations, which many college and university administrators are trying to put into place in order to advance straightforward institutional interests of their own— preserving diversity, teaching civility, preventing the loss of black undergraduates to other schools—generates a great deal of business for the ACLU and similar absolutist organizations. In a sense, the ACLU and conservative bigots are hand-in-glove. Like criminals and police, they understand each other's method of operation, mentality, and objectives. There is a tacit understanding of how each shall behave, how each shall gain from the other. Indeed, primarily because the Ku Klux Klan and similar clients are so *bad*, the ACLU gets to feel romantic and virtuous— and the rest of us, who despise racism and bigotry, are seen as benighted fools because we do not understand how the First Amendment really works.

But we do. The bigot is not a stand-in for Tom Paine. The best way to preserve lizards is not to preserve hawks. Reality is not paradoxical. Sometimes, defending Nazis is simply defending Nazis.

> "There's really something seriously wrong with the people who believe that it should be illegal to hurt a homosexual's feelings."

HATE SPEECH IS NOT A SERIOUS HATE CRIMES PROBLEM

William L. Pierce

William L. Pierce is the founder of the National Alliance, a white supremacist group. He also wrote, under the pseudonym Andrew Macdonald, *The Turner Diaries*. In the following viewpoint—taken from his weekly radio program that is published in his monthly on-line magazine *Free Speech*—he argues that those who protest against hate speech are really trying to ban any word or action that might offend someone. However, the U.S. Constitution does not guarantee people the right to not be offended, he asserts. Pierce contends that being free means permitting speech that may hurt some people's feelings so that the truth may be told.

As you read, consider the following questions:

1. According to Pierce, what is the only group that is not officially protected from hate speech?
2. How does Pierce's version of what *The Turner Diaries* is about compare to critics' versions?
3. According to the author, what are the only rights Americans have?

Reprinted from William L. Pierce, "Hate Speech," *Free Speech*, November 1995, by permission of *Free Speech*, PO Box 330, Hillsboro, WV 24946; www.natvan.com.

I've spoken often with you about the Jewish monopoly control of our mass media of news and entertainment. Recently I detailed the takeover of the Disney company by Jews and its conversion into an instrument of brainwashing used against young Americans.

In addition to this consolidation of Jewish control over the media, there's another subversive campaign underway in this country which is just as dangerous for our future. It's the campaign to stifle any expression of opinion except those coming from the Jew-controlled mass media: the campaign to outlaw all dissident voices.

When I've mentioned this campaign in the past, some people have thought I was being an alarmist. They believe that freedom of speech is too deeply rooted in American soil to be done away with by a few extremists in the Clinton administration, or any administration. The American people won't tolerate having their freedom of speech taken away, they believe.

TRYING TO OUTLAW OFFENSIVE SPEECH

I wish that I could share their optimism. What makes it difficult for me to do so is the fact that there is a growing body of opinion in America that no one should have the right to do or say anything which offends someone else. The people who believe this are not only entrenched in the Clinton administration, they're entrenched in the Congress, in the universities, and in many other American institutions. These people will tell you with a straight face that the First Amendment was never meant to protect offensive speech—or what they more often these days call—*hate speech*. The Constitution doesn't give anyone the right to hurt someone else's feelings, they say. It doesn't give anyone the right to offend someone else. It doesn't give anyone the right to say unkind things about someone else, so that other people might be influenced by what is said and then in turn think or say unkind things themselves—perhaps even do something unkind.

Actually, what these Politically Correct people really mean, although they won't tell you this—what they really mean is that no one should be permitted to write or say anything which might offend one of the officially favored classes of people: homosexuals, morally or physically defective people, Jews, Blacks or members of other non-White racial groups, and women. They see nothing wrong with offending a White male, for example: they do it themselves all the time. But they do believe that it ought to be illegal to do or say something offensive to almost anyone else.

A Victim of Political Correctness

Let me tell you about something which happened last month in Ottawa. I'm reading from a news article in the August 5, 1995, issue of the *Toronto Sun*. It says:

> A female Ottawa dentist who wore a facemask, gloves, and gown while treating an HIV-positive patient is facing charges of discrimination by the Ontario Human Rights Commission. . . . Medical history revealed that the patient was HIV-positive and had a past drug dependency, according to an Ontario Dental Association report. Before treating the patient in the two and one half hour visit, the dentist discussed with the patient her preference to wear a disposable gown, gloves, facemask, and eye protection while treating the patient. Following completion of the treatment the patient left without any negative comment about the care he received and booked for a six-month checkup.

That's the first part of the *Toronto Sun* story. The dentist and the patient talked things over before the treatment began; the dentist then put on her disposable gown, gloves, and so on to protect herself from the blood and saliva of the AIDS-infected patient; and after the treatment the patient left with no complaint.

But then one of the Politically Correct watchdogs of the Human Rights Commission heard about it, and things changed in a hurry. The *Toronto Sun* article continues:

> Both the Ontario Human Rights Commission and the Royal College of Dental Surgeons say in a report that the dentist acted in a discriminatory manner when she wore a paper gown in addition to her barrier protection gear, based solely on the patient's HIV status.

The news article went on to say that the dentist must not treat a patient with AIDS in any way differently from a healthy patient. If she doesn't wear a paper gown in treating healthy patients, then it is discriminatory to wear one when working on an AIDS-infected patient's teeth.

The article continues:

> The Ontario Human Rights Commission has threatened legal action against the dentist unless she complies with eight conditions, including paying the patient $8,000 to "compensate him for his mental anguish."

Well, you say, that was Canada, not the United States.

Let me tell you, the people of Canada are not really very different from the people of the United States. What they will let their government get away with now, we'll let our government get away with in five or ten years. America already is swarming with Human Relations Councils and Human Rights Councils, whose business it is to sniff out cases of AIDS carriers who have had their feelings hurt by some insensitive person who refused to treat them as if they were healthy. And believe me, every one of these Human Rights Councils in the United States is just itching to have the judicial power to order people locked up who say or do anything they don't like.

VISUAL HARASSMENT

I have another newspaper article in front of me, this one from the *Minneapolis-St. Paul Star Tribune* for July 23, 1995. It describes a ruling issued by an official of the Minneapolis city government, warning city workers that henceforth they may be disciplined for what the official calls "visual harassment." By "visual harassment" the official means looking at any female who does not want to be looked at. A woman had complained to the official, he said, that it made her "uncomfortable" that members of city work crews had stared at her as she walked past them. The name of the official who decided that such looking would henceforth result in disciplinary action is, believe it or not, Carl Markus. Not Marx, just Markus.

Now that would just be funny, if it were an isolated case. But things just as ridiculous, just as Orwellian, are happening every day in America. The people who want to get rid of the First Amendment—and the rest of the Bill of Rights too—the people who want to make it illegal to say or do anything which might offend an AIDS carrier or a feminist with a chip on her shoulder or whatever—are probing, pushing, trying to see what they can get away with, trying to see how far they can go, how much the American people will tolerate. The two articles I've quoted from today I chose as examples because of the air of absurdity to them which makes them a little catchy, a little memorable. But I have a hundred more news articles from the past few months which in more prosaic terms describe the same sort of efforts to outlaw offensiveness, or "hate," as it's often called.

HURT FEELINGS

Perhaps I should say at this point that I understand what it means to be offended and to have one's feelings hurt. I've worn glasses since I was five years old, and it used to hurt my feelings when some of my school classmates would call me "four eyes." I used to do pretty well in my school work too, and as a result occasionally one of the kids who didn't do so well would refer to me sneeringly as "Einstein." That really made me feel uncomfortable.

And I'm sure it's uncomfortable for a person who's overweight to hear herself called "fatso." I'm sure it makes a retarded person feel bad to be told he's stupid. I'm sure that a person who's not attractive doesn't like to be reminded of that fact.

But, you know, that's life. We all put up with a lot of things we don't like. We try to make the best of it. If we're fat and we don't like being called fatso, we try to lose some weight. If we're nearsighted and have to wear glasses, perhaps we can switch to contact lenses—or take karate lessons and punch out anybody who calls us "four eyes."

There's really something seriously wrong with the people who believe that it should be illegal to hurt a homosexual's feelings, or to stare at a pretty girl—or to call a person who wears glasses "four eyes," for that matter. Some of these people clearly believe that it's more important for us all to be able to feel good about ourselves all the time than it is for us to be free.

THE FEEL-GOOD FACTION

And some of these people are simply using the "feel-good" faction to push their own agenda, which is to make it impossible for the few people who have figured out what they're up to to tell the rest of the people. They want to make it illegal to tell people about the Jewish control of the news and entertainment media, for example. They want to make it illegal for this program to be on the air. They call this program "hate radio," because it is offensive to them.

What makes me worry so much is that the "feel-good" faction is growing. There's something unhealthy about life in America today, and it's making more and more people really believe that they have a right not to be offended or have their feelings hurt, and that that supposed right is more important than the right to free speech. And the folks who are taking advantage of this sickness by pushing the idea that offensive speech or hate speech ought to be outlawed are becoming more pushy in their efforts.

THE TURNER DIARIES

Back in 1978 I wrote a novel which I called The Turner Diaries. It's a novel about life in the United States as I imagined it might be in the 1990s, if some of the trends I could see in the 1970s continued for another 20 years. I imagined that the government would become more repressive, and it has. I imagined that most of the people would react in a sheeplike way to government repression and would not complain as long as they could still be comfortable and feel good, and that's the way it's turned out.

And I imagined that a few people would not react like sheep, but instead would fight back violently—and a few have. In writing my novel, I really tried to be realistic, and to speak my mind completely. I didn't rewrite any part of my book or leave out any part because I thought it might be offensive to some people—and, of course, it has been.

MORE SPEECH IS THE ANSWER TO HATE SPEECH

The First Amendment to the United States Constitution protects speech no matter how offensive its content. . . .

How much we value the right of free speech is put to its severest test when the speaker is someone we disagree with most. Speech that deeply offends our morality or is hostile to our way of life warrants the same constitutional protection as other speech because the right of free speech is indivisible: When one of us is denied this right, all of us are denied.

American Civil Liberties Union, "Hate Speech on Campus," 1996.

I have a clipping here from the July 14, 1995, issue of *The Jewish Press*, which is published in New York City and which describes itself as the world's largest circulation English-language Jewish newspaper. It's a story about what the folks at *The Jewish Press* see as a need to "close the loopholes in the U. S. Constitution," as they so nicely put it. And it's a story about the novel I wrote. I'll read you a couple of paragraphs from this story in *The Jewish Press*:

The radical right is taking advantage of the Republican victory in Congress to push its own agenda in defiance of the principles that have made the United States a haven for persecuted minorities, a beacon of freedom, justice, and liberty to all people. Unfortunately, the man-made laws under which we operate are like a two-edged sword, offering opportunity to all elements of society to achieve their goals but also similar rights for all to speak their minds even when it contravenes the very essence of tolerance and democracy. One glaring example of this attempt to exploit the loopholes in the U.S. Constitution to bring prejudice and racism in their most vicious forms to public attention is the publication in 1978 of a book called *The Turner Diaries* by Andrew Macdonald, the pseudonym of William L. Pierce, a former professor of physics and research scientist. . . . Pierce's book, which surpasses *Mein Kampf* in its virulent anti-Semitism, has sold more than 187,000 copies. It describes an end-of-the-century scenario in which the Jewish-dominated government is overthrown by the Organization, an underground white group which succeeds where Nazism failed. . . . Our first reaction . . . is that even in the

United States there must be a limit to such abuse of so-called freedom of speech. We have enough experience with vicious racists to justify some control over their actions.

Did you note the phrase "so-called freedom of speech"? These folks at The Jewish Press really would like for the government to prohibit the writing and publication of novels with plots they find offensive or hateful.

MAKING THE FIRST AMENDMENT OBSOLETE

I have another newspaper clipping, this one from the August 23, 1995, edition of the Fulton County Daily Report. It's an editorial written by two radical feminists, one a law professor and the other a law student at Northwestern University. Like The Jewish Press these two women also focus on my novel The Turner Diaries. They urge that the laws of our land be changed so that I and others who write books they find offensive can be prosecuted—or at least sued for the damage they claim our writing causes. In my case, they allege that the person or persons who blew up the federal building in Oklahoma City in 1995 were caused to do so by reading The Turner Diaries, and so therefore I should be sued for all of the deaths and property loss caused by that act. And, of course, the same for other books which they allege caused people to do harmful things or which offend people—and, believe me, these women and their friends on the Human Rights Councils are easily offended. And they are quick to see a cause-and-effect relationship between written words or an image in a book and criminal acts by people who read those words. They take it for granted that literature which they consider demeaning to women causes men to rape women. I'll read you just a little of their article:

> Even under current constitutional law, all speech is not equally protected regardless of content. The test is whether the harm caused by the speech is so grave that it outweighs the benefits of protecting its authors from liability. Usually the answer is no. This delicate balancing of interests, however, depends upon judgments about the severity of the harm, not on some absolute legal protection for all things written. Wrapping William Pierce in the fabric of the First Amendment ensures that there is a class of harms occasioned by violent and hate-filled images—insults, threats, beatings, rapes, and killings—that remain immune from ordinary legal consequence, even when cause and effect are plainly evident. In reality, if not in First Amendment theory, there persists a connection between image, incitement, and violence: cross-burnings and lynchings, yellow stars and deportations, pornography and rape, The Turner Diaries and Oklahoma City.

Well, it's pretty clear what these two feminists have in mind, even if they don't come right out and say it. They want to make it illegal for you or for me to insult or offend them or someone in solidarity with them—or, barring that, they want to be able to sue us for saying something which hurts the feelings of an AIDS carrier or a homosexual or a feminist or a member of one of the other officially protected minorities. They say, in effect, "Look, if we let William Pierce get away with writing books like *The Turner Diaries* just because of this obsolete legal fiction called the First Amendment, then we'll also have to put up with all sorts of other insults and hate-filled images."

I don't know what sort of insults have so rankled these two feminist lawyers, but it's pretty clear that they're rankled. I wouldn't worry about that so much, except that I'm afraid that the number of feel-good trendies who'll fall for their argument to abolish the First Amendment is growing. Worse than that, I worry that too many of the rest of us will just sit on our hands and let the anti-Constitutional lynch mob have its way.

TRYING TO REINTERPRET THE FIRST AMENDMENT

And, you know, politicians keep up with these trends too. They read the newspapers. They take polls. If they believe that the majority of Americans will fight to keep their rights, then the politicians won't mess with them. They'll even make speeches about how much they love the Constitution, and especially the First Amendment. But as soon as they figure that the people won't fight for their rights, they'll be leading the lynch mob and making speeches about the need to protect people from being offended or harmed by hateful speech.

And what I've just said applies to nearly all politicians and their camp followers, not just to the Clintonistas. It applies to Republicans and conservatives at least as much as it applies to Democrats and liberals. I have another newspaper article, with an essay by Robert Bork, the very conservative legal scholar who was hounded out of his Supreme Court nomination in 1987 because of his conservatism. Mr. Bork now says that we need to reinterpret the First Amendment, so that it does not protect hateful speech. I don't know what appointment Mr. Bork has his eye on now, but that's what the man is saying.

NO INALIENABLE RIGHTS

It all boils down to this: Nobody in this country, or anywhere else, has any *inalienable* rights: not the right to free speech or freedom of religion or assembly, not the right to keep and bear arms, not the right to be free from unreasonable searches and seizures. There always will be scoundrels who will try to take away your rights if they believe they can get away with it. And there always will be fools who will let them do it. The only rights that we have, the only rights that we can depend on, are those that we are willing and able to fight for, to shed blood for. And that's what it's coming to in this country very soon.

Now you've heard it. Now I want you think about it. And then I want you to start getting ready for what's coming.

PERIODICAL BIBLIOGRAPHY

The following articles have been selected to supplement the diverse views presented in this chapter. Addresses are provided for periodicals not indexed in the *Readers' Guide to Periodical Literature*, the *Alternative Press Index*, the *Social Sciences Index*, or the *Index to Legal Periodicals and Books*.

Howard Chua-Eoan	"Beneath the Surface," *Time*, June 22, 1998.
Richard Delgado	"Q: Do Prohibitions of Hate Speech Harm Public Discourse? No: Such Rules Make Campuses and Workplaces User-Friendly to All," *Insight*, June 24, 1996. Available from 3600 New York Ave. NE, Washington, DC 20002.
Christopher John Farley	"Kids and Race: A New Poll Shows Teenagers, Black and White, Have Moved Beyond Their Parents' Views of Race," *Time*, November 24, 1997.
William Finnegan	"The Unwanted," *New Yorker*, December 1, 1997.
Michael Fumento	"A Church Arson Epidemic? It's Smoke and Mirrors," *Wall Street Journal*, July 8, 1996.
Hamil R. Harris	"The Fires This Time," *Washington Post National Weekly*, July 1–7, 1996. Available from 1150 15th St. NW, Washington, DC 20071.
Michael Kelly	"Playing with Fire," *New Yorker*, July 15, 1996.
Jonathan S. Landay	"Rise in Hate Crimes Looms Behind Church Burnings," *Christian Science Monitor*, June 28, 1996.
Art Levine	"The Strange Case of Faked Hate Crimes," *U.S. News & World Report*, November 3, 1997.
Joshua Muravchik	"Facing Up to Black Anti-Semitism," *Commentary*, December 1995.
Dan Quinn	"The Crime That's Not Necessarily a Crime," *Advocate*, June 10, 1997.
Jonathan Rauch	"In Defense of Prejudice," *Harper's*, May 1995.
Kathi Wolfe	"Bashing the Disabled: The New Hate Crime," *Progressive*, November 1995.

CHAPTER 2

Do Certain Groups Promote Hate and Violence?

CHAPTER PREFACE

On June 6, 1998, James Byrd Jr., a forty-nine-year-old black man, was hitchhiking in Jasper, Texas, when three white men in a pickup truck offered him a ride. According to one of the men in the pickup, they drove to an isolated area where Byrd was beaten, then chained by his ankles to the back of the truck and dragged for over two miles on an asphalt road. Parts of his body were later found scattered along the road for over a mile. Three ex-convicts with suspected ties to white supremacist groups—Lawrence Brewer, Shawn Berry, and John King—were arrested and charged with Byrd's murder.

Nearly everyone familiar with Byrd's case, from the Texas Ku Klux Klan faction Knights of the White Kamellia (KWK) to the FBI, agrees that his murder was a hate crime. Morris Dees, founder of the civil rights organization Southern Poverty Law Center, contends that hate groups such as the KWK should be held morally, legally, and financially responsible for hate crimes committed by their members. "Even though they may not have told someone to [commit a specific crime]," Dees argues, "they told some of their local officials to use violence against minorities. In carrying that out, . . . it might be considered carrying out the direct orders of the Klan leaders."

The Knights of the White Kamellia deny, however, that Brewer, King, and Berry had any connection with the Klan. Darrell Flinn, imperial wizard of the KWK, argues that Byrd's murder was "a heinous crime that none of us in the [white supremacist] movement would orchestrate, condone, or even permit within our ranks. Brian Levin, director of the Center on Hate and Extremism in New Jersey, maintains that it is unlikely that the men would have been following orders from the Klan; 90 percent to 95 percent of hate crimes are committed by individuals, not hate groups, he asserts. John Craig, coauthor of Soldiers of God, agrees, adding that Byrd's murder was most likely "an opportunity crime" committed by three intoxicated white men with a chain in the back of the truck who found a black man alone on a country road.

The public outcry following Byrd's murder has focused attention on the influence of hate groups in promoting their racist goals. The authors in the following chapter examine whether certain groups promote hate and violence.

"Some white supremacists are opting to lead the way as a guerrilla strike force, precipitating the purification of America of all those who are not white, straight, and Christian."

WHITE SUPREMACIST GROUPS PROMOTE HATE AND VIOLENCE

Loretta Ross

In the following viewpoint, Loretta Ross argues that white supremacist groups are increasing their numbers and effectiveness by exploiting white fears about social change or racial differences. While white supremacist groups continue to direct hate-filled invectives against blacks and other minorities, she asserts, they are also targeting gays and lesbians, Jews, and women. To achieve their goal of a white, heterosexual, and Christian society, Ross maintains, white supremacists have turned to more violent strategies of hate. Ross is the founder and executive director of the Atlanta-based Center for Human Rights Education, a training and resource center for grassroots activists on using human rights to address social injustices.

As you read, consider the following questions:

1. How have the beliefs of white supremacists been transformed into "acceptable" mainstream values, in the author's opinion?
2. According to Ross, what is the fastest growing hate crime category in the United States?
3. What is the proportion of women in the membership of some hate groups, according to the author?

Reprinted, by permission, from Loretta Ross, "White Supremacy in the 1990's," *The Public Eye*, 1995.

The notion that racism is a violation of human rights is not a new one, as those who have experienced its effects would testify. The ground-breaking progress gained by the civil rights movement of the 1960s in the United States has steadily eroded over the past decade, and the issues and incidents of racism as well as anti-Semitism, homophobia, and violence against women are ones that need to be addressed with increasing urgency. While the courts are more and more frequently relying on civil rights laws to prosecute racially motivated violence, the common abuses of basic human rights are often overlooked. In fact, the encroachment of white supremacist ideologies into the social fabric of our politics, our institutions, and our laws means that intolerance is becoming the rule of the day, and the overt violation of the persons and property of individuals and groups is not only easily accepted, but part of the *status quo*.

America has moved into a new era of white supremacy. The new tactics used by white supremacists and far right organizations must be exposed so that we can work together to mitigate their effectiveness. . . . Racism cannot stand alone as the sole antagonist of human rights violations. The victims of white supremacist ideologies and politics include immigrants, gays and lesbians, Jews, and women, as well as people of color. . . .

SHIFTING TACTICS

When the New Hope Baptist Church in Seattle, Washington, was struck by arson in the spring of 1994, it was reportedly because its minister, Rev. Robert Jeffrey, is a progressive activist in the area. Jeffrey, an African American, is involved in fighting several anti-gay initiatives in the state. He is also a sponsor of Black Dollar Days, which organizes the African American community to spend its dollars exclusively with Black businesses. Many believe the attack on his predominantly Black church was intended to drive a wedge between African American and gay and lesbian forces in the region.

At the same time, a new computer bulletin board opened up in the area. Calling itself the "Gay Agenda Resistance," the electronic network offers its subscribers tips on how to stop the gay rights movement in the Pacific Northwest. With the right passwords, it also includes tips on how to target their opponents with violence.

Is this a coincidence? Probably not. What this story illustrates is how the white supremacist movement in America has learned to shift its tactics. No longer able to rely on open racism as an effective recruiting tactic, they have now found a more socially acceptable target for hate—lesbians and gays.

Is this a new white supremacist movement? Does this mean they no longer hate people of color, Jews, feminists, immigrants, etc.? No and No. The number of hate crimes in this country is evidence that hatred still exists as a family value.

A NEW STRATEGY

Hate groups are refocusing their energies. They are worried that they can never convince the majority of white Americans to join them in their netherworld. While many whites may share their prejudices, very few are willing to act on them by openly carrying a Klan calling card or an Uzi. This situation demands a new strategy that combines old hatreds with new rhetoric. White supremacists desperately need to reinvigorate their movement with new recruits by manipulating white fears into action.

White fears of change or difference are exploited by hate groups. At the same time, they are expanding their targets of hate. They have adopted not only homophobia as a prominent part of their new agenda, but are forcefully anti-abortion, pro-family values, and pro-American, in addition to their traditional racist and anti-Semitic beliefs. This broadening of issues and the use of conservative buzzwords have attracted the attention of whites who may not consider themselves racist, but do consider themselves patriotic Americans concerned about the moral decay of "their" country.

From the ranks of homophobes, anti-abortionists, racists, anti-Semites, and those who are simply afraid of a fast-changing world, white supremacists find willing allies in their struggle to control America's destiny. Hate groups cannot be dismissed as no more complex than the virulence of a few fringe fanatics. With the breathless way the media covers hate groups, it is sometimes easier to characterize them simply as misfits or extremists, rather than acknowledge them as part of the larger problem of widespread racism, anti-Semitism, and homophobia.

When they wish, hate groups get lots of free publicity from tabloid talk shows eager to boost ratings with the winning combination of race, guns, and violence. Such hosts may hypocritically hold their noses while racists, particularly skinheads, advertise their toughness and their addresses on national TV.

In this way, many more people are exposed to their message, convinced by their passion, and seduced by their simplistic answers to complex social problems. With time and repetition, white supremacists have fused many "fringe" far right beliefs together into "acceptable" mainstream values. While hate groups have previously relied on violence, their new manipulation of ultra-conservative rhetoric has combined with this to provoke a deadly acceptance of intolerance in this country.

TRYING TO STOP SOCIAL CHANGE

The influence of hate groups is evident in the increase in violent hate crimes across the nation. Most are committed not by actual members of hate groups, but by freelancers trying to halt the social changes around them. Many are trying to form hate gangs of their own.

FBI statistics report that 65 percent of America's hate crimes are committed by whites against Blacks. A good portion of such hate crimes are what we call "move-in" violence, when neighborhoods, schools, churches, or jobs are finally integrated 30 years after the 1964 Civil Rights Act. Terror over the visibility of the lesbian and gay movement lies behind the numerous hate crimes against gays and lesbians (and their allies)—the fastest-growing hate crime category in the country.

Some of the haters, living on the United States' borders, are petrified at the thought that brown hordes of Mexicans, Chinese, or Haitians may swarm over them if they cease their militant rhetoric and violence toward these immigrants. If they live near Native American reservations, the aim of their violence is to challenge the few remaining treaty rights granted native peoples.

Other white supremacists want to save the white race by controlling the behavior of white women—they attack interracial couples, lesbians, and feminists. They join the anti-abortion movement, believing they can prevent white women from getting legal abortions. Racist far right organizations have been quick to glorify anti-abortion violence, making it yet another hot issue to fuel the fires of the white revolution.

There are others who want to save the environment for the white race. They have infiltrated the environmental movement, or have switched sides to join the Wise Use movement. They are frantic to exploit the earth's natural resources to accumulate wealth before that time early in the 21st century when demographics predict that America will no longer be majority-white. In particular, many new recruits to the movement come from the Religious Right across a bridge of homophobia. Haters robed in clerical black are barely distinguishable from those hiding under white bedsheets, particularly in the eyes of their victims.

Hate groups have decided that they are no longer willing to wait for the white revolution—the violent backlash against human rights movements. They want a fast solution before, as they put it, "the white race is extinct."

Some white supremacists are opting to lead the way as a guerrilla strike force, precipitating the purification of America of all those who are not white, straight, and Christian. In a frank statement about white supremacist strategy, Aryan Nations member Louis Beam wrote:

> We do not advocate segregation. That was a temporary measure that is long past. . . . Our Order intends to take part in the Physical and Spiritual Racial Purification of ALL those countries which have traditionally been considered White lands in Modern Times. . . . We intend to purge this entire land area of Every non-White person, gene, idea and influence. [Capitalization in original.]

These self-described "white separatists" believe that the United States government is controlled by a conspiratorial cabal of non-whites or Jews, or a combination of both. They seek to change this "Zionist Occupation Government" either through terror or violence, or by influencing the political mainstream. They tell their followers that crime and welfare abuse by African Americans, immigration by Mexicans and Asians, or a fictional Jewish conspiracy are responsible for a decline in the status of white people. They accuse civil rights organizations of "hating white people" and brand whites who do not support them as race traitors or self-haters.

These fanatics are terrorists who use bombs, murder, arson, and assaults in their genocidal war. Some skinheads—for example, the Fourth Reich Skins arrested in 1993 in Los Angeles or the Aryan National Front, convicted of murdering homeless people in Alabama—are in the vanguard of this street-level violence. Meanwhile, older survivalists like Randy Weaver, who was acquitted of killing a federal marshall in an Idaho firefight in 1992, are barricaded in mountain shelters with stockpiles of weapons, awaiting the final Armageddon.

Impressionable, often alienated people, both young and old, are natural recruits for this movement. They bring new energy and a willingness to display their hatred aggressively. They also expand the influence of the white supremacist movement—into the anti-abortion movement, into the anti-gay movement, into the English-only movement—opening new avenues for the expression of hate.

BULLETS FOR BALLOTS

Other white supremacists are following a less violent strategy: exchanging bullets for ballots and running for political office. Some attempt to clone David Duke's success. With a little cosmetic surgery on the nose and resume, Duke [a former grand wizard of the Ku Klux Klan] was able to convince 55 percent of white Louisianians to vote for him when he ran for governor in 1992. Tapping into the resentment of the white backlash, Duke promoted himself as a defender of white rights and, for a brief moment, shook America out of its racial daydream.

HOLDING WHITE SUPREMACISTS ACCOUNTABLE FOR VIOLENCE

Tom Metzger, who [the Southern Poverty Law Center] sued in Oregon for the killing of an Ethiopian student in Portland, is a California white-supremacy leader with a group called the White Aryan Resistance. Before that, Metzger headed up the California Knights of the Ku Klux Klan. . . .

In the Metzger case, . . . here was Tom Metzger, who said, "I'm 1,200 miles away from this murder. I'm down in California. I didn't know the victim, and I didn't know the people who killed him. I'm just pushing my ideas about the superiority of the white Aryan race. That's my right, and you can't hold me liable because some skinheads read my stuff and took it on themselves to go kill a black person."

My trial theme was, "In America, you have the right to hate, but you don't have the right to hurt." We said Metzger stepped across the line. And that line was this: He sent an agent to Portland, and that agent testified for us that Metzger told him that the race war that they hoped would come one day would only come if they encouraged acts of racial violence.

Morris Dees Jr., Interviewed by Julie Gannon Shoop, *Trial*, January 1997.

Many observers were surprised so many whites voted for Duke since they had lied in pre-election polls. Duke set himself apart from other "klandidates" by convincing the majority of whites to act on their perceived group interests as whites— something that had not been achieved so openly since the 1980s' romance with the Reagan revolution.

What many Americans fail to realize is that, increasingly, white people are being literally scared out of their wits by demagogues like Duke, who crystallize for them their fears of people of color, lesbians and gays, the government, the media, welfare mothers, immigrants, the economy, health care—and the list goes on. Instead of rejecting Duke as a fringe opportunist, they voted for him because of his well-documented racist past. He was serious about white rights; he gave them permission to practice a kinder, gentler white supremacy.

In the 1990s, the image of organized hate is rapidly changing.

It is no longer the exclusive domain of white men over 30. It is becoming younger and meaner. Many people join the movement as teenagers, including a remarkable number of young women.

A kind of "Sisterhood of Hate" to procreate white supremacy has emerged. Since the mid-1980s, women have joined the racist movement in record numbers—from the White Nurses preparing for racial holy war to female skinheads producing videotapes on natural childbirth techniques. This new and dangerous increase accounts for nearly one-third of the membership of some hate groups. The increase in the number of women, coupled with a strategic thrust to reform the public image of hate groups, has expanded women's leadership.

These new recruits do not fit the stereotypical image of wives on their husbands' arms. In fact, many of them are college-educated, very sophisticated, and display skills usually found among the rarest of intellectuals in the movement.

THE IDEOLOGY HAS MUTATED

Most Americans don't understand the pervasiveness of white supremacists and the importance of their ideology in America's self-definition. Thus, they are unaware of how this ideology has mutated over the years and now blurs the lines between organized racists and their more mainstream counterparts in the Religious Right and ultra-conservative movements.

Of particular concern is a continuing convergence of sections of the white supremacist movement with the radical Christian Right, as represented by Pat Robertson, and nationalist ultra-conservatives, as represented by Pat Buchanan. This alliance is between religious determinists who think that one's degree of Christianity determines one's future, economic determinists who see themselves in a war of the "haves" against the "have-nots," and biological determinists for whom race is everything. All believe they are in battle to save Western civilization (white Europeans) from the ungodly and the unfit (people of color, gays and lesbians, and Jews).

Their cutting edge issue has been homophobia, as anti-gay campaigns have enriched their coffers and also mobilized a conservative current in the African American community. For example, their ability to oppose allowing gays in the military transferred directly to killing or stalling President Bill Clinton's proposals on the budget, health care reform, jobs, and economic recovery. Of the three trends, the ultra-conservatives have the best ability to mainstream their views. . . .

Election campaigns featuring isolationist and nationalist

83

themes and ultra-Christianity are an opportunity for rapprochement for all sectors of the right wing. They can march back to the center of power sharing a very big tent. No Special Rights and No Political Correctness campaigns have their origins in the white supremacist belief that white supremacy is right for America. . . .

FIGHTING WHITE SUPREMACIST GROUPS

Just because white supremacy exists and has done so for a long time, there is no reason for its victims to accept it. This apparent tautology serves as a reminder of the distracting potential for misdirecting our focus into fighting each other rather than understanding the nature and endurance of white supremacy. . . .

Together, we must hold, not only individuals, but governments accountable. The silence of government equals permission to hate. Local governments must be responsible for the abuse of basic human rights of its citizens. State governments must stand up against intolerance. And the federal government must be the guiding force behind the protection of human rights and human dignity in this country in which we claim that all are created equal. Local, state, and federal legislation must be enacted and enforced to protect individuals and groups from racial, religious, homophobic, and xenophobic intolerance.

The human rights community must also more thoroughly study and analyze the full extent to which white supremacist motivated human rights abuses occur in this country. The cost of racism, homophobia, anti-Semitism, sexism, and nationalism is high, not only to individuals but to whole groups of people who fall into certain "categories." Their victimization leaves them afraid in the streets, in their jobs, and even in their homes. Unable and unwilling to disguise the very essence of who they are, they face abuse ranging from mild intolerance to threat of death.

At the present time, there are not safe places for the victims of this type of violence to turn to. No homeless shelters, no women's shelters, and often even no police departments offer them support. The first step in building these resources is to recognize the magnitude of the problem so that human rights activists can come together to offer help and support to those outside the majority rule.

BREAKING THE CYCLE OF HATE

A concerted, prolonged effort to teach young people about the true impact of white supremacy and its prevalence in American society is fundamental to breaking the cycle. To ignore this issue is to build intolerance into the next generation. An understanding of the historical and institutional effects of racism and the other "isms" that dominate our culture and society is vital to understanding present bigotry and abuse.

When we recognize that racism, homophobia, sexism, anti-Semitism, and xenophobia flow from the same spring, and that they permeate every aspect of the lives of all Americans, we can then take steps together to make the United States a place that respects and honors the dignity of all people.

"*All of these media protests about the growth of hate in America are intended for the specific purpose of provoking hate.*"

ANTI-HATE GROUPS PROMOTE HATE

William L. Pierce

William L. Pierce is the founder of the white supremacist organization the National Alliance. In the following viewpoint—taken from his weekly radio program, which is transcribed and published in his monthly on-line magazine *Free Speech*—he rejects the media's claim that white supremacist groups promote hate and violence against nonwhites. The goal of white supremacist organizations such as the National Alliance is to protect and promote the welfare of white people, he asserts. Pierce contends that the media's false reports about the organizations' motives and actions incite hatred—the very emotion the media is censuring—against the groups' members. The real haters and promoters of violence are those who take the side of nonwhites in any conflict, he asserts.

As you read, consider the following questions:

1. What message are the media trying to send their audiences about white separatist groups, in Pierce's opinion?
2. Who feels the most threatened by the National Alliance's attempts to promote the welfare of the white race, according to to Pierce?
3. According to the author, why are the media biased against Germans?

Reprinted from William L. Pierce, "Who Are the Haters?" *Free Speech*, September 1997, by permission of *Free Speech*, PO Box 330, Hillsboro, WV 24946; www.natvan.com.

My organization, the National Alliance, concerns itself with all things relevant to the welfare and progress of the European peoples, the White people of this earth. We are advocates for all things which could be beneficial to our people, and we are opponents of all the influences and tendencies and groups who are harmful to our people. As a consequence of this we receive a certain amount of hate mail, and I find it interesting to read these hate letters and try to understand the psychology, the motivations, of the people who write them. I won't read any of these hate letters to you today, because they're all pretty nasty and tend to lean pretty heavily on the use of four-letter words. They also tend to be blindly and irrationally hateful and to be based less on what I actually have said or done than on some misrepresentation about me or the National Alliance which has appeared recently in the controlled media.

THE MEDIA PROVOKE HATE

In fact, there's a strong correlation between some sensational story appearing on television or in the *New York Times* or the *Village Voice* about the National Alliance being a so-called "hate group" and my novel *The Turner Diaries* being a "blueprint" for various acts of domestic terrorism on the one hand, and on the other hand the arrival of these hate letters at our office a few days thereafter. It is clear to me that these sensational stories in the controlled media, which all purport to be against hate—in fact, they claim to deplore the growth of hate in our society, to be alarmed about it, and to be seeking ways to ameliorate it—these stories denouncing hate have the effect of causing the arrival of hate letters at our office. There is a cause-and-effect relationship. And the more I've thought about it, the more I've become convinced that it was planned that way.

Which is to say, all of these media protests about the growth of hate in America are intended for the specific purpose of *provoking* hate, of inciting hate. If you collect these stories from the *New York Times*, *Time*, *Newsweek*, or other Jewish publications and study them, you'll see a certain pattern. For example, they always use the word "hate" in writing about me or the National Alliance. Even a short story may use the word "hate" or "hater" or the phrase "hate group" a dozen or more times. It's clear that this isn't just a fluke, because it occurs so consistently. What they're deliberately trying to do is create an association in the mind of the average reader or television viewer between any mention of me or my organization and the emotion of hatred. In fact, they not only want the listeners or viewers to reflexively think "hate" when they hear my name or the name of the National Alliance, they want them to *feel* hate. And it seems to work to a certain extent, judging from this correlation I mentioned between the appearance of these stories and the arrival of hate mail at our office.

It's an irrational, Pavlovian sort of thing, because as I mentioned a minute ago, the National Alliance is *not* a hate group of any sort but instead is a group dedicated to the welfare and progress of our people. But clearly there are folks out there who feel threatened by any such effort: folks who regard any activity aimed at building a sense of racial solidarity and racial consciousness among Europeans as a threat to themselves. And foremost among these folks are those who control the mass media: those who own the *New York Times*, the *Village Voice*, *Time*, *Newsweek*, and the rest. They are a deceitful bunch. They don't come right out and say that they are opposed to White people regaining an understanding of our roots and an appreciation for our own unique qualities in a rapidly darkening world and a sense of responsibility for the future of our people. They don't say this. Instead they attempt to generate negative associations in the minds of their mass audience. They attempt to use psychological trickery to keep our people confused and disorganized. They don't want us thinking clearly about what is in our own interest and what is not. They deliberately attempt to incite hatred against me and others who are concerned about the future of our people.

BIAS AGAINST GERMANS

They've had a lot of experience at inciting hatred. If you're a person of German ancestry, you'll certainly understand this. For the past 60 years, ever since the late 1930s, the media bosses have been cranking out films—hundreds of them—designed to incite hatred against Germans: crude, heavy-handed films, full of distortions and outright lies, but still effective enough to profoundly affect public opinion and national policy.

You may be better able to understand this media bias if you compare the films they have made about Germans with the films they have made about Japanese. You know, it was Japan who attacked the United States in the Second World War, not Germany. The Germans wanted to avoid a conflict with America and even ignored the deliberate provocations of the Roosevelt government, such as American attacks on German ships. After we were in the war, the Germans treated American prisoners correctly, in contrast to the Japanese, who often behaved brutally toward American prisoners, starving and torturing them. But the films coming out of Hollywood don't reflect this reality. For every anti-Japanese film there are a hundred anti-German films. In fact, Hollywood's tendency has been to generate sympathy toward the Japanese by reminding Americans at every opportunity about our internment of Japanese civilians in concentration camps in this country during the war. By way of contrast, the Germans are portrayed as sadistic automatons, clicking their heels and shouting "*Sieg Heil*" as they massacre prisoners.

THE JEWISH PROBLEM

Think about this difference between the Hollywood portrayal of Japanese and Germans. You won't have to think very long to understand that the reason the media bosses want to incite hatred against the Germans but not against the Japanese is based on the fact that the Germans were in the business of freeing their own country of Jewish influence and of fighting against Jewish Communism everywhere in Europe, while the Japanese were blessed by not having a Jewish problem to deal with. The media bosses, in other words, couldn't care less about the fact that the Germans treated American prisoners of war correctly and the Japanese didn't; all they care about is the way their fellow Jews were treated. That ethnic self-centeredness of theirs shows up in almost all of their propaganda.

For the last few years their hate propaganda has been directed not just at Germans, but also at everyone who is not Politically Correct—especially those groups like the National Alliance whose stand on the Jewish issue or the race issue differs from their own. And they have added a new twist: using a pretended campaign against hate to incite hate.

You know, I didn't think much about hate myself until becoming the target of this Jewish hate campaign. And then I had to ask myself, am I really a hater? Certainly not in the way the people who send those hate letters are. But, yes, I suppose I do hate some people.

A CAMPAIGN TO INCITE HATE AGAINST HATE

Whenever I look at what has happened to our cities and our schools since the 1950s and 1960s, I cannot suppress my feeling of hostility toward the Blacks, mestizos, and Asians who have made so much of our country an enemy-occupied wasteland. I feel a surge of anger every time I see a non-White face on television or in an advertisement. Thirty or 40 years ago, before all of the new civil-rights laws gave them a privileged status and when there were 25 or 30 million fewer of them in the country, I didn't feel this hostility. I figured that we could each stay in our own communities and we wouldn't get in each other's way. But now I want them out of our country, out of our living space. But even so, my hostility toward these non-Whites who are overrunning my world is not the nasty sort of hatred embellished with obscenity that I see expressed in the hate letters I receive.

A LOVE FOR THE WHITE RACE

What is the actual driving force behind the "racist" White Christian Nationalist's fight for the preservation of the Aryan Race? The news media would scream an immense and piercing shriek of "HATE" if they could catch the slightest whisper of such a question coming from ruddy Aryan lips. But those long standing warriors in this Struggle know that the answer has a much greater depth and meaning than the anti-Christ Jews, mongrel hordes and liberal White race-mixers could even begin to fathom . . . that of LOVE.

The depths of Love are rooted and very deep in a real White Nationalist's soul and spirit, no form of "hate" could even begin to compare.

Aryan Nations, "White Racism: Where Does It Come From?" No date.

When I see a hate letter I often feel a flash of anger at the hater who wrote it, but I cannot say that I really hate even these hate-letter writers. They are simply the people, most of them White, who are incited by the real hatemongers, the media bosses. My feeling toward these Jewish media bosses—and all of the clever, little Jewish propagandists who write news stories about so-called "hate groups" in an attempt to make ordinary people hate me—is much closer to real hatred. Over the years they have done enormous damage to our people with their poisonous propaganda, and they aspire to do even more. One way or another we must stop them and make sure that they can never harm our people again.

THE COLLABORATORS

But I reserve my most heartfelt hatred for the collaborators among my own people who make it possible for the Jews to do their damage: collaborators who consciously and deliberately betray their own people, lie to their own people, in order to gain advantage for themselves—the politicians, generals, public officials, clergymen, professors, writers, businessmen, and publicists who are not incited to hatred by the psychological tricks of the Jews, as are the suggestible fools who write hate letters, but who consciously and deliberately choose race treason, believing that they will gain a personal advantage from it. There is no fire in hell hot enough to punish these traitors, and there will be no place for them to hide when the day of retribution comes.

Yes, I hate traitors, I hate liars and deceivers, and I cannot say that I feel at all apologetic about the fact that I hate them. Hate may be an unpleasant sort of emotion, but it can serve a good purpose, and that is why Mother Nature gave us the capability to hate. It is one of the faculties which protects us from traitors and deceivers by ensuring that we will punish them, that we will weed them from our midst when we catch them, instead of forgiving them and giving them a chance to betray us again.

Nevertheless, I reject the label of "hater," with which the real hatemongers have tried to brand me. I spend very little of my time hating and a great deal of my time spreading understanding with the hope that it will benefit my people. One of the things I believe that we must understand, that we must always be aware of, is the motivation of the professional hatemongers, as well as the trickery with which they ply their trade.

A New Trick

Their trick of using the pretense of altruistically fighting hate in order to incite hate against their enemies is relatively new. They invented the terms "hate crime" and "hate speech" in 1990—unless one wants to give the credit for that to George Orwell, who popularized the essentially identical concept of "thought crime" in 1948, with his futuristic novel 1984. In any case, they used their political influence to force the government and the various police agencies around the country to give official recognition to their invention, or Orwell's invention if you prefer, with the passage of the so-called "Hate Crimes Statistics Reporting Act" of 1990. Then almost overnight all of the mass media began using the terms. Now they've got the President of the United States running around the country giving speeches about stamping out "hate crime" and "hate speech." It's their way of demonizing their enemies, of making their enemies seem like irrational, dangerous, and hateful people: the sort of people that it's all right for decent folks to hate.

So the trick is new, but the hate they bear against humanity certainly isn't new. Two thousand years ago the great Roman historian Tacitus noted as the principal distinguishing characteristic of the Jews their hatred for every nation but their own. This hatred they bear against other peoples may serve a useful purpose for the Jews by helping them to remain apart and to retain their own identity while existing as a small but influential minority among much larger host populations, but it certainly isn't helpful to our people. They almost instinctively are hostile to every institution of ours which holds us together and gives us our strength and solidarity. Back during the Vietnam war they were at the forefront of the flag-burners, and they persuaded a whole generation of university students and other young Americans to despise patriotism. Today their deceptive hate campaign is still directed against patriots, whom they portray as terrorists or potential terrorists.

POLITICAL CORRECTNESS

Consider the whole set of ideas and attitudes associated with Political Correctness. Political Correctness really has not been codified in any formal way, so that one can refer to some official proclamation in order to determine what is Politically Correct and what is not. Nevertheless, we all know. We absorb this knowledge from the mass media.

We know, for example, that the United Negro College Fund and the National Association for the Advancement of Colored People are Politically Correct. No one flinches or protests at the mention of those very real organizations. But at the same time we all know that if anyone dared to attempt to organize a college fund reserved for White students, he would be met with howls of outrage from the guardians of Political Correctness. We know that any association for the advancement of White interests will be branded immediately a "hate group" by the Jewish media and all of the politicians who dance to their tune, as the National Alliance is. In fact, any club or other organization with an all-White membership is bound to be under suspicion of being a "hate group," although the same suspicion is never directed against an all-Jewish organization, an all-Chinese organization, or an organization all of whose members are American Indians.

We all know that to express revulsion for the practices of homosexuals is the height of Political Incorrectness and will get us branded as "haters" in an instant. Even if we want to give our own children positive examples of heterosexual masculinity or heterosexual femininity in order to guide the development of their own attitudes toward sex, we had better do it quietly if we don't want to be accused of "hate." Likewise, any expression of support for the maintenance of traditional sex roles—any suggestion that armed combat is not a proper role for women, for example—is sure to bring one under suspicion as a "hater."

WHO THE REAL HATERS ARE

We all know that whenever White people, European people, are in conflict with non-Whites, whether in South Africa or America or anywhere else on this increasingly overcrowded planet, it is Politically Correct to be on the non-White side. To be on the White side is to be a "hater." If one expresses agreement with the French people who believe that the French government should cut off the immigration of Africans from the former French colonies in Africa, for example, one is a "hater." If one agrees with the Germans who believe that there are too many Turkish "guest workers" in Germany, one is a "hater." If one agrees with Englishmen that the Pakistanis in England should be sent back to Pakistan, one is a "hater." And if we suggest that the American government should not let wetbacks continue to pour into the United States across the Rio Grande, we are "haters." Indeed, only a "hater" would dare use the term "wetback" these days.

If we are sufficiently sensitive to the message of the controlled media, we understand that any expression of concern for our people, any effort to safeguard the future of our people, any public support for our traditions and our culture and our folkways is hateful. The unspoken message is that we will be hated if we are not Politically Correct. The message is that the sort of trendy fools who send me viciously obscene hate letters will be incited to hate anyone who does not toe the political line of the Jewish media.

It's a shame that it still has to be that way for a while yet. It's a shame that any of our people are incited to hate others of our people. But we have a big mess to clean up in America and elsewhere throughout the White world, and until the mess has been cleaned up there will be hatred.

At least, we can understand who is responsible for this hatred. We can understand who the real haters are.

> "Organized hate groups are not the main perpetrators of violent acts; individuals are."

INDIVIDUALS ARE RESPONSIBLE FOR MOST HATE CRIMES

Jack Levin and Jack McDevitt

Jack Levin and Jack McDevitt argue in the following viewpoint that most hate crimes are not committed by "true believers" of hate groups whose mission is to eliminate people of a despised group from the world. Instead, they contend, individuals who are motivated by their own personal prejudice are responsible for most hate crimes. More research is needed to study the motivations of people who commit hate crimes, the authors maintain. Levin is a professor of sociology and criminology at Northeastern University. McDevitt is codirector of Northeastern University's Center for Applied Social Research. Levin and McDevitt are the authors of *Hate Crimes:The Rising Tide of Bigotry and Bloodshed*.

As you read, consider the following questions:

1. How does the number of skinheads in the United States at their peak in the 1980s compare to the number of skinheads in Germany, according to the authors?
2. What are the three motivations behind hate crimes, in the authors' opinion?
3. According to Levin and McDevitt, why have researchers played down the importance of prejudice in motivating individuals to commit hate crimes?

Reprinted, by permission, from Jack Levin and Jack McDevitt, "The Research Needed to Understand Hate Crime," *Chronicle of Higher Education*, August 4, 1995.

The April 19th, 1995, bombing of a federal office building in Oklahoma City has drawn our attention to the growing threat of organized hate groups' spreading terror and disrupting the fabric of American society. Since the Oklahoma tragedy, several suspects were linked to radical right-wing organizations that share a belief in white supremacy.

Militias and neo-Nazi and other white-supremacist groups are growing at an alarming rate, according to Brian Levin of Klanwatch, a national organization that monitors the activities of hate groups. Unfortunately, we know very little about these organizations—or about the prejudices that motivate them. To date, behavioral scientists have conducted very little research on the activities of white-supremacist organizations.

We do know that throughout the 1980s membership in almost all hate groups, including the Ku Klux Klan and the White Aryan Resistance, either remained stable or declined. During this period, only the number of youthful skinheads, sporting steel-toed boots, black leather jackets, shaved heads, and racist attitudes, increased. But even at their peak, in the mid-1980s, American skinheads numbered only 3,500 at most, in a population of more than 250 million. (To put this figure in some perspective, Germany has 30,000 racist skinheads in a population of 78 million.)

We also know that membership in local militia groups opposing the power of the federal government has begun to grow, and that a number of influential white supremacists have become involved in the armed-militia movement. This merger of racism and anti-federalism has appealed to some Americans looking for someone to blame for their considerable economic problems.

As we saw in Oklahoma City, hate groups can be dangerous. While their conspiratorial views and excessive secrecy make it difficult to study them, academic researchers must begin to estimate their numbers, budgets, influence, and plans for the future. At the same time, researchers must be careful not to let the Oklahoma bombing distort their understanding.

We have analyzed 450 incidents that occurred in Boston in the late 1980s and 4,000 that occurred nationwide in 1990 that can be classified as hate crimes. The results show that organized hate groups are not the main perpetrators of violent acts; individuals are. Our research suggests that up to 95 per cent of all crimes in which the victim was chosen because of a particular characteristic, such as race, religion, ethnicity, gender, disability, or sexual orientation, are acts of individual bigotry—perhaps partially inspired by, but not necessarily committed by, the members of any organization.

We have found that perpetrators of hate crimes can be categorized by their motivation. The majority—roughly two-thirds—
of them are "thrill seekers," often bored and alienated young-
sters looking for excitement in bashing or assaulting someone
who is different. In some cities, Asians and Latinos face the
greatest risk of becoming victims; in others, gays and blacks do.

A second category of hate crimes can be regarded as "defensive"—they are directed against a particular set of "outsiders"
(most frequently blacks, Asians, or Latinos) who have moved
into a previously all-white neighborhood or onto a predominantly white college campus. In our research, we found that a
little more than one-third of the crimes fell into this category.
Once again, the perpetrators were typically not attached to any
organized hate group, but were individuals who feel personally
threatened by the presence of newcomers who "don't belong."

The third and rarest type of hate crime—less than 1 per cent
of the total—is carried out by "true believers," members of organized groups who perceive themselves to be victims of some
conspiracy and claim to have a "mission" to rid the world of another, despised group. The activities of militias that espouse a
white-supremacist ideology fall into this third category.

Unfortunately, we know very little more about what motivates
people to carry out hate crimes—whether individually or as
members of hate groups. During the 1970s, psychologists and
sociologists conducted a great deal of research on prejudice (although not on hate crimes *per se*). They sought to discover why
some people are prejudiced against blacks or Jews, for example,
and what psychological ends the prejudice serves. Such research
could easily have led to the present-day study of hate crimes.
However, since the 1980s, scholars increasingly have played
down the importance of prejudice in motivating individuals.

PREJUDICE

In 1974, for example, 55 academic-journal articles in psychology and 32 in sociology dealt directly with the concept of prejudice. By 1984, the figures had declined somewhat, to 41 articles in psychology and 26 in sociology. By 1994, only 30
psychology articles and 13 sociology articles were concerned
with the topic of prejudice.

The reason is that, until very recently, many researchers have
argued that prejudice, such as racial bias, is decreasing. They
point, for example, to the fact that the proportion of white
Americans who say they believe that blacks are inferior has de-

clined steadily since the 1960s. So, rather than focus on how prejudice motivates individuals, they have turned their attention to the way it is institutionalized.

They have looked, for example, at how college admissions have been skewed by the Scholastic Assessment Tests, which indirectly favor white applicants, and at how real-estate associations "steer" black homebuyers away from white neighborhoods. The personal biases of particular admission officers or real-estate agents have been ignored. However, while behavioral scientists have enthusiastically examined such issues, hate violence and harassment perpetrated by individuals have increased dramatically.

THE PEOPLE BEHIND HATE CRIMES

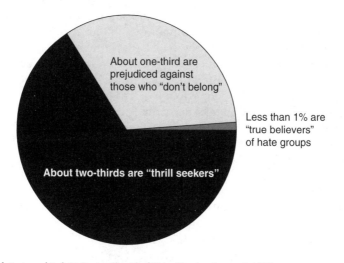

About one-third are prejudiced against those who "don't belong"

Less than 1% are "true believers" of hate groups

About two-thirds are "thrill seekers"

Jack Levin and Jack McDevitt, *Chronicle of Higher Education*, August 4, 1995.

Based on a national survey, in 1990 Louis Harris reported that more than half of all high-school students claimed to have witnessed racial confrontations either "very often" or "once in a while." The Prejudice Institute of the Center for the Applied Study of Ethnoviolence, at Towson State University, reported an upsurge during the late 1980s in racial and anti-Semitic episodes on college campuses. It estimated that 20 per cent of all students from racial and ethnic minority groups were either physically or verbally harassed during their college years. (The figure approached 30 per cent for anti-Semitic incidents in 1989.) And a survey of 55 colleges conducted by *U.S. News & World Report* found that 71 percent of the institutions had had at least one such incident reported during the academic year 1992–93.

INFORMATION IS INADEQUATE

The rise in expressions of hate is not, of course, restricted to our schools and colleges. The Anti-Defamation League's 1994 figures for the nation as a whole showed an 11-per-cent increase over the previous year in anti-Semitic incidents. Moreover, according to Klanwatch, the number of bias-motivated assaults resulting in physical injury to Americans increased from 183 in 1993 to 228 in 1994. Many of those attacks were directed at gays or lesbians.

We know that much. But the information available concerning incidents of bias-motivated violence still is woefully inadequate. For example, we don't know if the kinds of prejudice that motivate people to carry out hate crimes are held by only a few people or by many. Is a man who joins a hate group an angry white male, with much in common with other men around the country? Or is he more likely to be a psychotic white male, motivated by very specific personal factors? We need to focus not only on the size or location of hate groups, but also on individuals, to discover why people join hate groups in the first place.

How should researchers proceed? Police departments supply data on hate crimes that we can use; advocacy groups, such as the Anti-Defamation League and the National Gay and Lesbian Task Force, also provide such data. Unfortunately, the police data may be unreliable, because victims of hate crimes, even more than crime victims in general, often are afraid to report such attacks to police. And, although useful to those who study hate crimes, data collected by advocacy groups also may be unreliable, because such groups often lack the financial resources to investigate allegations.

RECOMMENDATIONS

To collect data about hate crimes and the prejudices that generate them, we urge the establishment of an independent national survey of hate crimes and victims. In collecting data, those preparing the survey should distinguish between actual crimes and other incidents (for example, verbal attacks) that harm victims but are not criminal. Data on hate crimes could be collected in the semiannual National Crime Victimization Survey conducted by the Bureau of Justice Statistics. At present, that survey fails to distinguish hate crimes from other criminal offenses.

We also recommend that colleges and universities be required to include a separate accounting of incidents motivated by hatred or bias in the now-mandatory annual report of campus-crime statistics.

However, better data is not enough. We also need to refocus the questions we ask. Institutional discrimination is probably as important as it ever has been. But we should realize that individual prejudices are often behind discrimination at the institutional level; think of how a bigoted college-admission official can use racial differences in S.A.T. scores to exclude students who belong to minority groups.

MORE RESEARCH IS NEEDED

Above all, more research is needed on the people who commit hate crimes. We should look specifically at the types of individuals who are susceptible to the recruiting efforts of organized hate groups. Future research should focus on discovering what kinds of people are likely to act out their prejudices in a violent manner, and which ones are the most likely to go along with peer pressure to attack vulnerable victims. We also need to look at the effectiveness of various alternative-sentencing programs in rehabilitating offenders.

Recent research contains hints of what a study of prejudice might find. Some results suggest that prejudice increases as society becomes more diverse. Howard J. Ehrlich, director of Towson State's Prejudice Institute, has found that group conflict attributable to growing diversity on college campuses is on the rise. In an era of declining opportunities and resources, college students tend to view classmates from different backgrounds as competitors rather than partners.

Research on hate crimes conducted at Yale University by the political scientist Donald Green and the psychologist Richard Abelson similarly supports the hypothesis that drastic changes in the ethnic or racial composition of a community are accompanied by a rise in such crimes.

As our nation has become more racially diverse, and as economic competition has become more intense, prejudice seems to have become more acceptable in our culture. Rap and heavy-metal lyrics express themes of violence and bigotry. On stage, "attack comics" aim their savage barbs at gays, women, immigrants, and people of color. It is past time to begin intense, systematic study of just what is going on.

"The only places and where [violent
bigots] can legally get a gun,
bayonet or baton and occasionally
use them to maim or kill is in a
law enforcement agency or the
military."

THE MILITARY ATTRACTS VIOLENT BIGOTS

Carl Rowan

In the following viewpoint, syndicated columnist Carl Rowan
argues that racism and bigotry in the armed forces is a serious
problem. He contends that people with violent, authoritarian
personalities are attracted to the military where they are given
weapons and trained to kill people. Federal investigations into
racism and hate groups in the military are merely an attempt to
appease angry voters, he maintains. The only way to eliminate
hate in the military is to court-martial and imprison the offenders, Rowan asserts.

As you read, consider the following questions:

1. Why is Rowan doubtful that the federal investigation into
   hate groups in the military will result in any real action?
2. What is the "Good Ol' Boys Roundup," according to the
   author?
3. How does Rowan counter the defense that the First
   Amendment permits hate groups in the armed forces?

Reprinted from Carl Rowan, "Who Can Rid the Military of Hate Groups?" Liberal Opinion,
January 1, 1996, by special permission of King Features Syndicate.

The coldblooded murders of a black man and woman near Fort Bragg, N.C., allegedly by three white soldiers who identify themselves as neo-Nazi skinheads, has aroused fears about the influence of hate groups in the U.S. military. Prodded by President Bill Clinton, Army Secretary Togo D. West Jr. has ordered a worldwide investigation of "extremists" and any "climate of hate" among our GIs.

The killings of Michael James, 36 and Jackie Burden, 27, as they simply walked down a street in Fayetteville, N.C., is chilling. Especially when the murders allegedly were committed as a lark by half drunken bigots who had volunteered and sworn to protect the American people. I know that President Clinton and West are serious.

Still, I truly doubt that anything of substance will be done to cleanse our military of skinhead, Ku Klux Klan, Aryan supremacy, anti-Semitic and anti-gay groups that will murder at a whim—and even blow up federal buildings, as may have been the case in Oklahoma City in April 1995. I can't believe that black GIs will not also be drawn into this wretched circle of hate and violence.

Two Reasons for Pessimism

My pessimism arises from two things:

1) The cells of hatred within armed forces reflect a dangerous increase in organized hatred in the American community at large—an increase inspired by politicians who over the last 20 years have made bigotry respectable, if not fashionable, again.

When racial segregation was at its worst (in the military and society at large) in 1944, I was a guinea pig black officer on a Navy ship in the North Atlantic. I faced nothing that compares with the venomous, organized racial and ethnic assaults that weaken our military today.

2) Federal investigations usually are weak pretenses of bureaucratic action designed to pacify worried or angry voters until they forget what they were upset about. We almost always get heap much talk and little action where racism is the problem.

A "Sickening" Event

Do you remember that in May 1995 we were shocked by revelations about an orgy of racism by law enforcement officers at a "Good Ol' Boys Roundup" in Tennessee. White officials and ordinary agents of the FBI, the Secret Service, the Customs Service, the Drug Enforcement Administration, the U.S. Marshals Service, the Internal Revenue Service, the Immigration and Naturalization Service, the Bureau of Prisons, and even the District of

Columbia Metropolitan Police would gather in Ocoee, Tenn., hiding behind a "Nigger Check Point," to get drunk and vent their racism. Employees of the Bureau of Alcohol, Tobacco and Firearms (ATF) had begun this event, called "sickening" by President Clinton, in 1985.

Reprinted by permission of Joe Sharpnack.

ATF Director John W. Magaw and the heads of the other law enforcement agencies promised "investigations" in July 1995. Even though there are videotapes of some of their employees attending those "roundups of hatred," we haven't seen a single report of any punishments being meted out to anyone.

It's time we faced the fact that some people—white, black, brown, or whatever—have violent, authoritarian personalities. The only places and where they can legally get a gun, bayonet or baton and occasionally use them to maim or kill is in a law enforcement agency or the military. We know about the crisis they have brought to the policing of America's cities. We are learning, much too late, of the frightening problems these authoritarians, especially those driven by hate, are bringing to our legitimate military—and to the "militias" that are springing up.

THE FIRST AMENDMENT IS NO PROTECTION

Secretary West's investigators will find that the haters will try to hide behind the First Amendment, arguing that rights of "free speech" entitle them to be skinheads, Klansmen or whatever in their "free time," and to spread wide their "literature" of hate. We have had it established before that a military unit is not a democracy. Free speech does not permit privates to argue with generals about what to do or not do in Bosnia. Nor does or should it permit sergeants or admirals to undermine military units by their spewing of hatred or their acts of wanton violence.

Investigations are meaningless until some asses get kicked and some courts-martial are held, and some brigs are loaded with neo-Nazis. Only that kind of action will ensure us a reliable military.

"Extremist activity in and on and touching the United States Army is minimal."

THE MILITARY DOES NOT ATTRACT VIOLENT BIGOTS

Togo D. West Jr.

Togo D. West Jr., the secretary of the Department of Veterans Affairs, was the secretary of the army from 1993 to 1998. After three white soldiers shot and killed a black couple in Fayetteville, North Carolina, in December 1995, West commissioned a study of extremist behavior in the army. The following viewpoint is excerpted from a press conference he gave in March 1996 explaining the results of the study. He asserts that an extremely low number of soldiers know of or are members of an extremist hate group. Hate groups have a very low presence in the army, he maintains, because most soldiers are firm believers in the traditional American values that are antithetical to hate groups.

As you read, consider the following questions:

1. According to the report cited by West, what percentage of soldiers know of extremists in uniform?
2. What reasons does West cite to explain why so few American soldiers are members of hate groups?
3. What prevents the army from prohibiting soldiers to have any association with hate groups, according to the author?

Reprinted from Togo D. West Jr., Press Conference, March 21, 1996. Available at www.defenselink.mil/news/Mar1996/t032196_ttogo032.html.

O n December 15th, 1995, I announced the establishment of the task force on extremism in the Army. I announced it in the wake of events in Fayetteville, North Carolina, which were a shock to our nation, and which caused us in the Army to decide that we needed to take a look at ourselves. [On December 6, 1995, Jim Burmeister Jr. and two other white soldiers, all self-described neo-Nazis, shot and killed a black couple who were taking a walk.] . . .

I named [the task force report] *Defending American Values* for I think obvious reasons. The fact is that the United States Army does not belong to me or to the Secretary of Defense. As proud as we are of them, it does not belong to our soldiers or our noncommissioned officers (NCOs) or our officers. It belongs to the American people. And as such, it should espouse the values of the people to whom it belongs. If it does, then it can defend them. That is our job. . . .

The task force concludes that this Army does indeed exemplify and wholeheartedly support American values. It concludes that extremist activity in and on and touching the United States Army is minimal. It concludes that there has been little in the way of targeting by extremist organizations or groups of U.S. Army soldiers. And it concludes that America can be as confident of its Army today as it has always been in the years past. . . .

The task force report offers us several findings. . . . I will mention only a couple of them, highlight them for you. With respect to . . . the some 7,000 interviews [conducted by the task force around the world], the task force finds that less than one percent of those interviewed . . . report knowing or coming into contact with extremists in uniform or [who are] family members or . . . civilians on that post. . . . Substantially less than one percent.

It also finds that these soldiers report—less than one percent, but a bit closer—report any contacts with media or other paraphernalia or literature of extremist or hate groups. The most often cited contact with any kind of insignia is the swastika or the initials KKK. . . .

EXTREMIST ACTIVITY IS MINIMAL

The conclusion that . . . the task force reaches . . . is that extremist activity in, around, or touching the Army is minimal. Now, we can say it in a lot of different ways, but I give it to you bare bones—minimal. Minimal means that our soldiers report little of it. Minimal means that there is little evidence of it. Minimal means that law enforcement officials around the base agree with those judgments.

Secondly, I would highlight for you with respect to extremist activities the panel reports that targeting—and I said this at the outset—targeting of active duty Army soldiers [by white supremacist or other racist groups] is simply not happening in any significant way. There may be several reasons for that. . . .

SOLDIERS ARE NOT GOOD TARGETS

It may well be that our soldiers are simply not good targets. That inoculated with the values of America, believing in what they defend, they are simply not easy prey. It may be that our soldiers are simply too busy. They train every day. They have important jobs to do. Most of our soldiers, the vast majority, simply don't have the time to go disaffected and to go seeking a family outside the Army which takes up so much of their time, so many hours of the day, so many days of the week, so many weeks of the year.

And the third perhaps most elevated reason may be simply that the soldiers aren't there long enough. They come, maybe they're assigned there for two or three years, and they move on. It may be that . . . there are such groups out there in significant strength to have a coherent plan of targeting—I doubt the latter, but if there are—that the targets would not be folks who, when you consider it, really are simply not available that often in the community to be targeted.

Thirdly, the task force reports . . . that our soldiers, in the vast majority, embraced the notion that extremism has no place in military life. That in short, our soldiers embrace the values of our citizens. That extremism has no place in American life. . . .

A CONSTANTLY CHANGING ARMY

Over 21 percent of our force changes every year in the active force. One-fifth of our Army goes and comes every year. . . . And probably another two-fifths at any given point has been on active duty less than four years. That has been an Army that has good news and bad news. It is an Army that is very . . . reflective of the values of society. It is also an Army that still needs some training about how the Army takes those values of society, improves upon them so that we get a higher level of performance for our soldiers. There may be extremism out in America. We simply cannot use it in the Army.

The final conclusion that I would call to your attention . . . is a kind of extra-added attraction. If we ask our soldiers in this brief look-see—this brief investigation of the Army—"Well, what concerns you the most in this whole area of potential trouble on the borders of our installations or people making inroads into our Army?" The answer is gang-related activity near or on our posts. As large a percentage of our soldiers responded on that question as they responded on the extremism question. They said that they are concerned about security concerns and other issues arising from that phenomena. We don't confirm that there's a large presence. The task force doesn't confirm that there's a large presence. Law enforcement authorities don't confirm that there's a large presence, but our soldiers are concerned about it. It is something we need to take into account. . . .

A Need for a Continual Reassessment

I would say, that if there's a lesson or a message to draw from all this, it is that our soldiers, yes, are relatively untouched by extremism; but that we are on guard not to relax. There was some comment from some of the seminar respondents from the senior officers that maybe we in the Army are so proud of what we've done over the last 20 or 25 years since the early seventies, late sixties, about the human relations atmosphere in our Army that we think it's doing well, almost running on automatic.

Not a Conducive Environment

As the *New York Times* has grudgingly admitted, careful scrutiny of the Army has turned up "only a few hints of hate groups" like the Klan or neo-Nazi skinheads. In fact, the Army may be less afflicted by such groups than the public at large. Sociologist Rafe Ezekiel of Harvard University, a specialist in the study of the white supremacist movement, told the *Christian Science Monitor,* "The Army is not a climate conducive to hate-group membership. It's not so easy to be obscure in the military, and also there are a lot of noncommissioned officers who are blacks, so that gets in the way. It's really an integrated society." Ezekiel pointed out that the recruiting standards of the volunteer military tend to "squeeze out" potential hate group recruits.

William Norman Grigg, *New American,* January 22, 1996.

I hesitate to endorse that notion. I don't think any of our senior officers or junior officers or NCOs are running on automatic. But I am willing to accept the warning that we need to continually reassess ourselves. There are probably two basic elements to the kind of success we want in our Army: First-rate soldiers, and careful monitoring of what we're doing to support them. We've got those two elements. I think we're all right.

We've got the first-rate soldiers. The best in the world. We are reminded by this report that we must continue to introduce the other element, a continual reassessment, a re-look at our equal opportunity policies and all the things that go with it. If we do those well, we'll be all right in the end. Today's challenges will be remarked upon tomorrow as tomorrow's successes. With that, I'm available for your questions. . . .

THE FIRST AMENDMENT

Q: The report says that most soldiers believe that any association with an extremist organization should be grounds for separation from the Army. Why not simplify it in that way and eliminate the distinction between passive and active participation? Just say any association and you're out. Why not do that?

A: The First Amendment. What has, I think, motivated our lawyers in the past have been the First Amendment considerations, the process of drawing the current regulation based on the current Department of Defense (DoD) directive. As Judy Miller, the current general counsel of DoD, described to me just two days ago, it's painful and quite difficult. We have competing interests on both sides. We have sensed that even soldiers, regimented and uniformed as they are, still have some basic entitlements and the competing notion that says, for purposes of maintaining good order and discipline in our units, so that they can perform their missions, we can go very far indeed in what we proscribe.

That competition is what has resulted in the current Army Regulation. I do not say that our lawyers and personnel specialists won't come up with a way to do just what you said and just what the soldiers say. But I do say in answer to your question why might it not happen because we have to balance those two things.

Nonetheless, we are going to look at this very carefully, and my directions are there must be something better we can do with our regulation. We must be able to say more clearly what our idea is. What we prohibit. What we don't like. What is antithetical and we can certainly do that, whatever the conclusion, on just how much you can prohibit.

PERIODICAL BIBLIOGRAPHY

The following articles have been selected to supplement the diverse views presented in this chapter. Addresses are provided for periodicals not indexed in the *Readers' Guide to Periodical Literature*, the *Alternative Press Index*, the *Social Sciences Index*, or the *Index to Legal Periodicals and Books*.

Brian Britt	"Neo-Confederate Culture: A Culture of Pride and Bigotry," *Z Magazine*, December 1996.
Midge Decter	"The ADL vs. the Religious Right," *Commentary*, September 1994.
Sara Diamond	"Patriot Games," *Progressive*, September 1995.
Samuel Francis	"Witchfinder: The Strange Career of Morris Dees," *Chronicles*, November 1997. Available from the Rockford Institute, 934 N. Main St., Rockford, IL 61103-7061.
Henry Louis Gates Jr.	"The Charmer," *New Yorker*, April 29–May 6, 1996.
Tony Horwitz	"Rebel Voices: The Face of Extremism Wears Many Guises—Most of Them Ordinary," *Wall Street Journal*, April 28, 1995.
William F. Jasper	"Fabricating a Smear," *New American*, November 25, 1996. Available from 770 Westhill Blvd., Appleton, WI 54914.
Johnny Liberty	"Hate Crimes Perpetuated by Human Rights Organizations," *Free American*, June 1996. Available from PO Box 2016, Tijeras, NM 87059.
Michael Lind	"America's Scofflaw Conservatives," *Washington Post National Weekly Edition*, May 8–14, 1995. Available from 1150 15th St. NW, Washington, DC 20071.
Christopher Phelps	"The Christian Coalition, the Republican Party, and the Far Right: The Right's New Dynamism," *Against the Current*, September/October 1995.
Daniel Voll	"A Few Good Nazis," *Esquire*, April 1996.
Gordon Witkin	"Pride and Prejudice," *U.S. News & World Report*, July 15–22, 1996.
Don Wycliff	"Why Farrrakhan Appeals," *Commonweal*, November 17, 1995.
Mortimer B. Zuckerman	"Louis Farrakhan's White Noise," *U.S. News & World Report*, November 6, 1995.

DOES THE MILITIA MOVEMENT PRESENT A SERIOUS THREAT?

CHAPTER PREFACE

In August 1992, near Ruby Ridge, Idaho, federal law enforcement agents surrounded the secluded mountain home of Randy Weaver, who was wanted for selling illegal arms to an undercover agent. During the shoot-out that followed, Weaver's fourteen-year-old son and his dog were killed as they ran toward the cabin; his wife, who was holding their infant daughter in her arms, was also shot and killed as she stood in her home's doorway. Eight months later, in Waco, Texas, officers from the FBI and other agencies invaded the heavily armed compound of a religious sect to arrest the leader on weapons charges. The compound caught fire and eighty-six members of the Branch Davidian cult—including twenty-five children—were killed.

Many people maintain that the events at Ruby Ridge and Waco are indicative of the federal government's contempt for the rights of its citizens. Chief among these believers are militia groups, many of whom have a deep and abiding mistrust of government. Many militia members believe that the federal government is illegally expanding its power over American citizens and that people's constitutional rights—especially their property rights and their right to bear arms—are threatened by this expansion. The only way to fight this erosion of their rights, militia supporters contend, is to be vigilant against government excess and prepared to defend their rights with violence, if necessary.

Critics of militia groups believe that the April 1995 bombing of the federal building in Oklahoma City—which killed 168 people, including more than a dozen children in the building's daycare center—proves that militias are a dangerous threat to America. The bombing occurred two years to the day after the siege at Waco, and the two men convicted of the bombing—Timothy McVeigh and Terry Nichols—had ties to militia groups. Many militias stockpile weapons; opponents assert that this hoarding of arms, along with their stated intentions to use them, justifies using strong measures to suppress such groups.

The public response to these three incidents—Ruby Ridge, Waco, and Oklahoma City—illustrate the debate that swirls around militias. Militia supporters argue that the groups are necessary to protect their constitutional freedoms. Opponents maintain that militias threaten the safety and security of society. The authors in the following chapter examine whether the militia movement presents a serious threat to society and the government.

> "This is not merely a movement of gun-nuts running around in the woods on weekends in camouflage uniforms. It is a dangerous movement."

THE MILITIA MOVEMENT PRESENTS A SERIOUS THREAT

John M. Swomley

John M. Swomley is professor emeritus at the St. Paul School of Theology in Kansas City, Missouri. He also serves on the national board of the American Civil Liberties Union and chairs its church-state committee. In the following viewpoint, Swomley asserts that the militia movement is connected to racist and white supremacist groups, anti-abortion terrorists, and other organizations of the extreme right-wing. Leaders of militias and similar groups openly advocate violence and train their members in the use of firearms, Swomley argues. Even more frightening, he maintains, is that the U.S. government and federal agencies do not appear to be taking this threat seriously.

As you read, consider the following questions:
1. According to the author, in what three ways can militias be categorized as an arm of the extreme right?
2. What examples does Swomley give of what he sees as reluctance on the government's part to deal with right-wing militias?
3. What types of groups does the FBI keep under surveillance, according to Swomley?

Reprinted, by permission, from John M. Swomley, "Armed and Dangerous: The Threat of the 'Patriot Militias,'" *The Humanist*, November/December 1995.

The rise of the so-called patriot or citizens' militias has provoked a great deal of debate and concern. Reportedly forming in some 40 states, these militias have depicted themselves as grass-roots citizens groups which have banded together to defend against the threat of an increasingly powerful and lawless central government. But what kind of politics do the members of these militias espouse—and do they, in fact, represent a far greater threat to democracy than the government they are preparing to combat?

AN ARM OF THE EXTREME RIGHT

I would argue that there are at least three ways in which the various patriot militias can be categorized as an arm of the extreme right. The first is the use of intimidation and violence by members of these militias against local, state, and federal officials (especially women). In the June 7, 1995, New York Times, columnist Bob Herbert reported a seizure by federal agents of a computer disk, the contents of which were to be published by a Virginia militia group in its newsletter. The text read in part:

> Hit and run tactics will be our method of fighting . . . we will
> destroy targets such as telephone relay centers, bridges, fuel stor-
> age tanks, communications towers, radio stations, airports, etc.
> . . . Human targets will be engaged when it is beneficial to the
> cause to eliminate particular individuals who oppose us (troops,
> police, political figures, snitches, etc.).

A second reason to categorize the militia movement as an arm of the extreme right is its connection with racist or white supremacist groups, anti-abortion terrorists, and various other extremists. Marc Cooper, writing in the Nation about the Montana Militia (which he describes as "in many ways, the Mother of all militias"), reports that "at a closed-door meeting in the Rocky Mountains in October 1992 some 174 hard-right activists were brought together by the explicitly racist Christian Identity minister Pete Peters." One result of that meeting was the formation of the United Citizens for Justice, "led by former Texas Klan leader Louis Beam." Other leaders of the group included several members of the Montana Militia, including John Trochman, who founded the group with his nephew Randy and who is described by Cooper as "a participant in Aryan Nations' activities." There are numerous other connections between the militias and right-wing extremist groups such as the anti-environmental Wise Use movement, the Counties Movement, and neo-Nazi organizations.

A third reason to categorize the militias as an arm of the extreme right is their connection to certain "Christian" organizations and leaders. These include the Christian Reconstructionists, who advocate death for abortionists, homosexuals, and others; Randall Terry, founder of Operation Rescue, who has been supporting the growth of local militias; and Pat Robertson, whose book The New World Order sounds the alarm against the United Nations, an integral part of the militias' antagonism to the U. S. government. For both Robertson and the militias, the New World Order and the United Nations have replaced communism as the demonic ideological threat to American nationalism.

Like their allies in the Christian right, the militias are anti-abortion, anti-homosexual, and tend to accept fundamentalist, white-supremacist, and anti-Semitic theology, as well as the subordination of women. There is also an overlap between the militias and other groups influential with right-wing leaders in Congress, such as the National Rifle Association (NRA), whose interpretation of the Second Amendment's reference to "the right to bear arms" and "militias" is an important underpinning of the militia movement.

THE ANTI-ABORTION CONNECTION

Leaders of the violent wing of the anti-abortion movement are now related not only to other extreme right-wing movements but to armed militias. The Reverend Matthew Trewhella, leader of the new U.S. Taxpayers Party (USTP), has called for church-based paramilitary training. In a speech to the Wisconsin state convention of USTP before the April 1995 Oklahoma City bombing [in which a suspected militia member bombed a federal building, killing 169 people], he said: "We should do what thousands of people across this nation are doing. We should be forming militias. . . . Churches can form 'militia days' and teach their men how to fight."

Trewhella, whose congregation is primarily composed of people calling themselves Missionaries to the Preborn (formerly a branch of Operation Rescue), told the USTP convention that his Mercy Seat Christian Church in Milwaukee holds classes for its members on "the use of firearms and . . . how to be a good shot." Trewhella's language also matches that of the militias. He denounced the "traitors in Congress" and others in the federal government as "low-life swine" and "totalitarian dogs" who "want to see our country overthrown, and we have a duty to oppose these dogs."

Randall Terry has also advocated the use of violence. In his book The Sword: The Blessing of Righteous Government and the Overthrow of

Tyrants, he presents his vision of a theocratic revolution. In an April 10, 1995, meeting in Kenner, Louisiana, sponsored by Operation Rescue, he said: "There is going to be war." Christians may be called upon to "take up the sword" in order "to overthrow the tyrannical regime that oppresses them."

Terry also promoted his new Christian Leadership Institute, which he called a "Christian retreat for male leaders" that will generate "fierce, militant, unmerciful warriors." It would train leaders "to rebuild America's power bases on the foundation of the Ten Commandments," which means "a culture based on biblical law." His theocratic state would abolish public schools (because they usurp "parental guidance"), property taxes (which are the basis for financing public education), and prisons (which he would replace with "biblical slavery," public floggings, and the execution by stoning of rebellious teenagers).

According to Terry, leadership is "defined as the ability to get people to do things they don't want to do." He also said of his Christian Leadership Institute: "We'll be talking about not how to recapture government schools but how to utterly eliminate them." His faculty includes his pastor, the Reverend Daniel J. Little; leaders of the radical right U.S. Taxpayers Party; Joseph J. Slovenec (who got 28,000 votes in a third-party effort to become a U.S. senator from Ohio in the 1994 election); and Howard Phillips, who founded USTP in 1990.

Another anti-abortionist terrorist is convicted clinic bomber, the Reverend Michael Bray, who interprets "the biblical doctrine of revolution" in *A Time to Kill*, published by Advocates for Life Publications. He points to scriptural evidence, such as Samson's "one man guerrilla war against the Philistine government" and the "posse of men" led by Gideon, who overthrew the pagan Midianite government.

EXTREMIST GROUPS

Another extremist anti-abortion group is Human Life International (HLI) with 84 branches in 56 countries. The HLI supports the efforts of Operation Rescue, and its leader, Father Paul Marx, has been accused of anti-Semitism after having charged the Jews with not only condoning but more or less leading "the greatest holocaust of all time: the war on unborn babies." Marx has also opposed the rights of women, gays and lesbians, Muslims, and people with AIDS.

Even many prominent Catholics have recognized the inherent danger of such extremist groups as the HLI. In a Catholic News Service report for March 6, 1995, Monsignor George G. Higgins called the HLI "a divisive force within the pro-life movement" and the Catholic church.

The HLI's featured speaker at its 1994 world conference was Randall Terry, who received standing ovations when he challenged his audience to rise up and make America a "Christian nation under biblical law."

These various terrorist anti-abortion groups are involved with each other and are also related, through USTP, to other right-wing groups and to the militia movement. The USTP of Wisconsin, for example, is distributing a field manual, *Principles Justifying the Arming and Organizing of a Militia*. In it are such passages as:

> Eight men make an effective house assault team. While four men give suppressive fire, the other four can advance on and enter a house or small building. Once inside, two men may enter and clear rooms while the other two provide security in the hallway or open areas. . . .

> Combat cells provide the patrolling and fighting capability of the Free Militia. Each cell consists of about eight able-bodied "minutemen" with its own leader, communications, rendezvous points, staging areas and standing orders. They execute the orders of their command and do all their own training within the combat cell itself. They are the "arms" of the Free Militia.

TURNING A BLIND EYE

There has been a reluctance on the part of right-wing lawmakers in Congress to curb right-wing extremists such as the militias. Republicans in Congress have held hearings on both [the April 1993 incident in] Waco, Texas, [where more than 80 members of David Koresh's Branch Davidian cult died after a standoff with federal agents] and the August 1992 Randy Weaver incident [in which a shoot-out with federal agents in Ruby Ridge, Idaho, resulted in the deaths of Weaver's wife and teenage son] but, as of this writing, have refused to conduct extensive hearings on the militia movement. The events at both Waco and Ruby Ridge have become a rallying cry for the militias because they illustrate government violence against citizens because of their ownership and collection of arms.

The reluctance to deal with right-wing militants is also evident in government agencies like the FBI. During congressional hearings following the Oklahoma City bombing, FBI director Louis Freeh alleged that the FBI had not investigated or engaged in surveillance of the various militias because they had not been violent or broken the law. Freeh said, as reported in the May 3, 1995, *Washington Post*: "For two decades, the FBI has been at an extreme disadvantage with regard to domestic groups that advocate violence. We have no intelligence or background information on them until their violent talk becomes deadly action."

Yet for years the FBI has collected "intelligence" or background information on *nonviolent* groups which are either centrist or left of center. In 1994, the Center for Constitutional Rights (CCR) requested data under the Freedom of Information Act (FOIA) on 15 organizations, including ACT UP, Clergy and Laity Concerned, and Jewish and pacifist organizations. The CCR received information from the FBI concerning six of these 15 groups.

ACT UP, a relatively recent organization, has a file of 199 pages; the American Jewish Committee and the American Jewish Congress each have about 1,000 pages. The International Ladies Garment Workers Union totals 5,600 pages. However, of the 15 groups, the only organization committed in policy and practice to nonviolence since its origin in 1915—the Fellowship of Reconciliation (FOR)—has the largest file with 11,000 pages, according to the May 16, 1995, *New York Times.*

The New York FBI office claims that most of the files were gathered years before their guidelines were revised in 1976 and 1983. However, a reply to a 1991 FOIA request filed by the FOR revealed that the FBI file then contained 9,200 pages. Thus, the FBI has added 1,800 pages on the FOR between 1991 and 1995.

In short, the FBI winks at armed and dangerous right-wing groups and keeps under surveillance nonviolent centrist and left-wing groups which have never been a threat to anyone. No wonder that the FBI was caught flatfooted following the Oklahoma City bombing, because it had not been collecting information on potentially violent right-wing groups such as the various so-called patriot militias.

BLOCKING INQUIRIES

The Republican-controlled House and Senate are similarly unlikely to conduct public hearings that would expose Republican extremist fringe groups like the militias, Operation Rescue, and a host of other anti-abortion and gun-toting groups which have advocated or engaged in violence. In the June 7, 1995, *New York Times*, Bob Herbert wrote: "Mr. [Newt] Gingrich is blocking the kind of Congressional inquiry that would throw a badly needed spotlight on paramilitary activity in this country."

After a perfunctory Senate subcommittee hearing on June 15, 1995, which gave militia leaders the opportunity to assert that they are "law-abiding, God-fearing Americans" who pose no threat to anyone, seven House Democrats held an informal hearing on July 11, 1995. At the hearing, federal, state, and county agents described the threats to their lives they had received as they attempted to enforce the law. One county recorder in Stanislaus, California, said that, after she told a local man she lacked the authority to dismiss a tax lien against him, she found a pipe bomb under her car.

Lest anyone think that the militia movement is confined to Montana or Michigan or is chiefly an isolated phenomenon, it is important to note that militias exist in numerous communities, even though in some their membership is small. For example, the *Kansas City Star* listed Kansas and Missouri militias both in major cities (such as Topeka, Kansas City, St. Joseph, Springfield, and St. Louis) and in rural areas.

One of the major aims of the militia movement (as well as the NRA, Christian Coalition, and allied groups) is to elect public officials. One of those—Republican Helen Chenoweth of Idaho, who was elected to Congress with the help of the Idaho Militia—now openly espouses her organization's cause in Congress. This is not merely a movement of gun-nuts running around in the woods on weekends in camouflage uniforms. It is a dangerous movement, even though there undoubtedly are some (or many) in it who would not by themselves endanger the lives of others.

> "The government and the . . . media invoke the specters of . . . militias to frighten Americans into signing away their freedoms."

THE MILITIA MOVEMENT DOES NOT PRESENT A SERIOUS THREAT

Husayn Al-Kurdi

In the following viewpoint, Husayn Al-Kurdi argues that the potential threat of the militia movement has been exaggerated by the U.S. government and the media. Most militia members are middle-class Americans who fear that their rights are being encroached upon by an increasingly powerful federal government, according to Al-Kurdi. However, he maintains, the government has promulgated the belief that militias are dangerous organizations in order to build support for the restriction of gun ownership and other measures designed to weaken civil rights. The author concludes that both liberal and conservative Americans should unite to protect their civil liberties from further infringement. Al-Kurdi is the senior editor for News International Press Service and a widely published writer.

As you read, consider the following questions:

1. What is the main goal of militia supporters, according to Al-Kurdi?
2. What examples does the author give of "militias" that were active in the 1960s and 1970s?
3. In Al-Kurdi's opinion, where can the major terrorism be found?

Reprinted, by permission, from Husayn Al-Kurdi, "Strange Bedfellows: The Truth About Militias," *Perceptions*, August/September 1996.

Since the April 1995 Oklahoma City bombing [of the Alfred P. Murrah Federal Building], a domestic U.S. political movement has joined the long-time preferred targets from the Islamic and Arab worlds on the U.S. government list of enemies.

The "militia" movement has arisen in recent years to contest what it sees as the growth of government power within the domestic jurisdiction of the United States itself. Often referred to as simply "the militias," this movement consists of mostly middle-class, predominantly but not exclusively white Americans who are more than disgruntled with what they perceive as arbitrary and even tyrannical misrule by their own government.

CONCERNS OF MILITIA SUPPORTERS

Spokespersons for the "militias," who also occasionally call themselves "patriots," cite the attack at Waco, in which government forces besieged and assaulted a religious group in Texas, killing more than a hundred people in 1993, as evidence of a government gone wild with unregulated power. They also point to a long list of other assaults and killings including the 1992 siege and assault on Randy Weaver's family in Idaho, which resulted in the murder of his wife and child, and the 1992 murder of millionaire rancher Donald Scott in Malibu, California, by the Drug Enforcement Agency in an apparent bid to seize his property under drug laws. These people are straight, usually conservative Americans who bridle at government oppression and control and who see themselves as the inheritors of the American revolutionary war slogan, "Don't Tread on Me."

The militia supporters see and fear the erosion of their rights, including their right to keep and bear arms. Their main goal, as they see it, is the preservation of the U.S. Constitution, which they refer to as the single mandate of their movement. Widely portrayed as having links with white supremacist organizations such as the Klan, they vigorously deny such allegations and point to a growing number of black participants in the movement, including some in leadership roles. They seem to be a loosely federated movement with a presence in all 50 states, in urban as well as rural areas.

Many of these folks are concerned that their children or relatives may be forced to fight and die in some U.N. "peacekeeping" adventure whose goals are as remote from their interests and the actual interests of the overwhelming majority of the American people as some of the prospective terrains in which these operations are carried out (Middle East, Asia, Africa and Latin America). They espouse a belief in self-reliance and hold the populist notion that the people in arms are not nearly the threat that the State and federal governments have become.

"Militia" is most simply defined as any army or armed force composed of citizens rather than professional soldiers. All armed insurgent and guerrilla groups are forms of militia. Fidel Castro's band in the Sierra Maestra is a famous example, but no more so than the citizen groups who opposed the British at Lexington and Concord two centuries earlier. The reader will recall that the founding fathers of the United States considered "[a] well-regulated militia, being necessary to the security of a free State" (Second Amendment to the Constitution). Frantz Fanon, apostle of Third World liberation, saw the formation of the militia (the people armed) as being the guarantor of revolution and the check to the rise of arbitrary power internally as well as the ever-present threats emanating from what is now called the "world community."

The Changing Faces of Protest

This time, rebels and "revolutionaries" challenging the major power turn out to be from the Right, insofar as the Left/Right spectrum still has any meaning. Many of those pushing for "tough" State-sponsored measures (which those on the receiving end would probably with justification call "terrorist") now include voices from what calls itself the "progressive community," the remnants of what used to be called "the Left." Today, they cheer police repression against their opponents, exposing their own political opportunism, just as many in the other camp did in previous eras. The Pastor Martin Niemöller scenario evoked during the Hitler period has begun playing itself out once more. This time around, it begins "First they came for Randy Weaver's family and the Branch Davidians . . ."

Historically, "militias" have formed under a wide variety of circumstances. The Deacons and the Black Panthers appeared in black communities in the 1960s, largely to defend themselves from external armed forces such as the Klan and the police whom they saw (and see) as an occupying force hostile to the welfare and interests of law-abiding residents.

Of course, urban gangs are also a sort of "militia," and the government often tries to nullify, co-opt or destroy all such groups. Richard Nixon invited members of the Blackstone Nation to his inauguration, seeking to enlist the remnants of their legendary "Blackstone Rangers" in his drive to destroy the Black Panther Party and other forces in the burgeoning black-liberation movement. Much of the hullabaloo about "gangs" today reflects the elite's concern to control and direct the violence, not to eliminate it, and to prevent any one group from getting "out of hand" anywhere, certainly not to the point of challenging government legitimacy or jurisdiction.

GOVERNMENT OPPOSITION

In another example of group-vs.-group strategy, the U.S. government subsidized a "militia" to assist it in suppressing the American Indian struggle for self-determination in South Dakota. It organized and sponsored the G.O.O.N., "Guardians of Oglala Nation," led by Dick Wilson, to wipe out the militia of the American Indian Movement (AIM). Scores of AIM supporters were butchered in a blood bath which destroyed the movement.

The Black Panthers and the (Puerto Rican) Young Lords were among the many groups similarly destroyed in the FBI COINTELPRO [counter-intelligence propaganda] operations of the Sixties and Seventies. Ron Karenga's "US" organization was manipulated by the government against the Panthers. Armed or not, political movements are often crushed militarily when they present a threat to the status quo.

THE REAL THREATS

You want threats to the fabric of society? Consider the breakup of the American family with its hordes of unmarried mothers, illegitimate children and deadbeat fathers. Consider the 14-year-old gun-toting gang members or the thousands of dope dealers. Consider the collapse of our education system or history's most expensive failure—the federal war on poverty.

Compare these to a few isolated groups of worried, frustrated men and women preparing for the American Armageddon. They don't bother me.

Lyn Nofzinger, Insight, September 25–October 2, 1995.

The Chinese "Great Proletarian Cultural Revolution" engaged numerous armed student groups. There were "red sorts, black sorts and gray sorts," with the "Great Helmsman," Chairman Mao, directing the "sorting out" process. Today's fledgling street "gangster" would probably adapt quickly to the codes, handshakes, hand signs and rituals which the reds, blacks and grays used to sort out their affiliations. As Fulang Lo, a vigorous participant in the Cultural Revolution, recounts in her book Morning Breeze, there was even a "loyalty dance" which it was advisable to know. She tells us, "It was not difficult—just stretching your hands toward the sky and then drawing them back to your stomach to symbolize the idea that Chairman Mao was the sun rising from the heart to the sky." A lot of "mad doggin'" and even plenty of killing went on during the Cultural Revolution. The Chinese people suffered much then as they have subsequently, while their government "sorted" itself out.

Of course, the term "militias" also includes the Klan and the Sahara Club in California whose activities oppose civil liberties and human rights. The Sahara Club is a bunch of bikers who are angry because they can't have free access to the desert to practice their crudities. They target "environmentalists," publishing "hit lists" of activists in their newsletters. Some of them carry guns. Others take relish in beating up stray environmentalists. Some vigilante groups associate with industry against workers, often being hired and organized by the companies themselves, and have intermittently battled with workers' self-defense militias and those supporting worker strikes.

The labor unions seem to have definitely lost their struggle against the government and the corporations for which it stands. This is a country in which as much as a trillion dollars has been looted by private interests in the savings and loan bankruptcies and related events. A silenced majority with access only to state-controlled information and education is the preferred scenario for policy makers. Their prime strategy is borrowed from mushroom growers: Keep them in the dark and cover them with plenty of (fertilizer).

THE THREAT OF REPRESSIVE GOVERNMENT

Probably the only "militia" that we have to worry about in the near and distant future is the State's and the interests it serves. From the Left, Massachusetts Institute of Technology (MIT) Professor Noam Chomsky identifies the current American system and the actual dictatorship which has accompanied

> [T]he rise of corporations, (in fact) a manifestation of the same phenomena that led to fascism and bolshevism, out of the same totalitarian soil. The others have declined or been partially destroyed. This one is stronger than ever.

With an avalanche of repressive legislation in Congress continuing to erode civil rights, it would be wise, for once, to identify just where the real threat is located. "Left" and "Right" people would do well to condemn government attacks against their respective opponents.

Although he does not seem to be particularly concerned with the threat of government grabbing and regulating guns, Chomsky does sound a note of cautious optimism for change. He described the present as "an organizer's paradise," where large numbers of people are looking for positive answers to a broad range of social problems, with a worsening economic situation spurring on a possible period of intense political ferment. He went on to say that "There's no reason for (this system) to exist. There's no limit to the changes that can be made if people actually undertook the hard work of organizing instead of sort of staring out in misery at what is happening." For Chomsky, as for the "militias" and a broad array of others, the enemies of the people are social domination and the authoritarian and hierarchic structures that oppress people. If we can overcome (or at least set aside) our differences and distastes for each other, the possibilities for real change will improve. This requires learning the habit of overcoming all sorts of prejudices.

AMERICA CAN CHANGE

Above all else, we must undergo an education process, sometimes painful, exposing our own realities to the scrutiny which transforming them requires. Unlikely and hopeless as the proposition must seem to so many here and abroad, America can change—and radically. That may be in the best interests of the overwhelming majority of people both here and around the world, "Left," "Right" and all "sorts." That is the idea whose time has come, which no army or "militia" can defeat.

The government and the disturbingly compliant media invoke the specters of "terrorist" Muslims and militias to frighten Americans into signing away their freedoms and protections against an overreaching government, as guaranteed by the Bill of Rights and the Constitution. We must not be fooled. We must hope, for all of our sakes, that the most powerful force in the history of the world will be stopped—the U.S. government and its associates and "militias"—before the American people and countless others elsewhere are victimized further.

The black, brown and red people under its rule have suffered the most horrific holocausts in human history; that is where the major terrorism can be found. That wolf keeps crying "wolf" at Muslims and militias alike, and CNN and the other major media outlets continuously parrot the line that some small country or political group is fearsome. Meanwhile the major powers, led by the United States, keep advancing their world-ordering plans through terrorism and break their own records for genocide, with people of color becoming the grim statistics which enhance their "prestige."

> "The militias constitute a new
> manifestation of violent hate-group
> activity that ... target[s] ... any
> representative of government."

THE MILITIA MOVEMENT THREATENS
THE GOVERNMENT

Kenneth S. Stern

The militia movement poses a serious threat to the government,
Kenneth S. Stern asserts in the following viewpoint. According
to Stern, the militias frequently single out government officials
as targets for intimidation, harassment, and violence. Furthermore, he contends, militia members in many areas have gained
a stranglehold on local government proceedings by intimidating
local officials and frightening away citizens who would otherwise take part in community meetings and the political process.
It is essential to confront the danger that militias present to the
proper workings of civil government and to take steps to defuse
the movement, Stern concludes. Stern is a program specialist on
anti-Semitism and extremism for the American Jewish Committee in New York. He is also the author of *A Force upon the Plain: The
American Militia Movement and the Politics of Hate*.

As you read, consider the following questions:

1. According to Stern, how many people are connected with the
   militia movement?
2. What examples does the author provide of anti-government
   beliefs held by many militia members?
3. In the author's view, what is the likely result of the militia
   movement's blend of anti-Semitic and anti-government
   paranoia and guns?

Reprinted, by permission, from Kenneth S. Stern, "Militia Mania," *USA Today* magazine,
January 1996.

A well-armed and dangerous anti-government militia move-ment has been spreading with lightning pace across the country. Organizations and researchers who monitor this move-ment maintain that militias have either direct or indirect con-nections with organized white supremacists and are using the Internet, faxes, national shortwave radio, and videotapes to share their information and warfare training exercises. The militias constitute a new manifestation of violent hate-group activity that does not target only the traditional victims—racial and reli-gious minorities—but any representative of government or any-one perceived is opposing the militia and, therefore, seen as do-ing "the work of government."

TARGETING GOVERNMENT OFFICIALS

Militia members on the Internet claimed they were going to march on Washington and arrest Congress at gunpoint. An alert was issued by one group calling, not only for the arrest of mem-bers of Congress, but also their "trial for Treason by Citizen Courts." According to the *Arizona Republic*, "a militia group ob-tained the names and home addresses of all federal officers [in Mississippi], prompting U.S. agencies to post a nationwide alert."

Some estimates suggest that there are more than 15,000 people connected with the militia movement in over 40 states. People associated with militias have shot at police officers; gath-ered to try to down a National Guard helicopter; and been ar-rested in armed confrontations (one in an armed raid on a courthouse by people whose accomplices were waiting outside with assault rifles with bayonets, thousands of rounds of ammu-nition, radio equipment, plastic handcuffs, and $80,000 in cash, gold and silver, as well as bogus $3 bills with Pres. Clin-ton's portrait); and calmly explained how they might need to kill government officials.

Even after such acts, militia members apparently feel comfort-able enough to have their meeting notices listed in local papers. A Montana mayor aligned with this movement even declared his town a "freeman enclave" and then deposited $20,000,000 in bogus "freeman" money in a local bank.

INTIMIDATION

The threat of militia violence has frightened citizens away from participating in the political process. A Montana newspaper re-ports that "Some residents, fearing for their safety, have stopped attending [land use and other community] meetings altogether, allowing a vocal minority to dictate public policy." Mike Murray, a county commissioner in Montana, indicates that "We were . . . advised by law enforcement authorities that it's not wise to have our addresses listed in the phone book. . . . Sadly, people who want to be involved in government are being discouraged from participating, so we're losing the best and brightest we've got." A member of a California militia told his audience, "If your board of supervisors tries to do something you don't like, show up. They're going to assume someone in the back has a rope."

Some militias maintain they have connections to local law enforcement and military personnel, and say they are training with heavy weaponry stolen from U.S. military installations. Because militias are a threat to law and order, because they are organized around the country and are using the national communication systems for organizing, it is imperative that this movement not be viewed as a localized problem, but as a national one.

THE BACKGROUND OF THE MILITIA MOVEMENT

White supremacist and anti-Semite John Trochmann formed the Militia of Montana in February, 1994. Since then, similar groups, directly or indirectly connected to the white supremacist movement, have cropped up around the country. Hundreds of people have attended meetings, even in small communities. Many of these, including truck drivers, accountants, housewives, lawyers, farmers, doctors, loggers, and barbers, are preparing to fight the government because they believe their freedom is at stake.

Cited among their reasons are claims that the government laid siege to the Branch Davidians at Waco, Texas, and attacked white supremacist Randy Weaver in Idaho, as well as that the United Nations is expanding its military role. They oppose the Brady Bill. ("Gun control is for only one thing," militia members insist, "people control.") Some speak of government plans to shepherd dissidents into 43 concentration camps. (Mysterious numbers on the back of road signs, some say, are for this purpose, or for providing information to invading troops.) Others claim that the government plans to murder more than three-quarters of the American people; that unmarked black helicopters are poised to attack them and sometimes threaten people by focusing lasers into their eyes; that Hong Kong policemen and Gurka troops are training in the Montana wilderness in order to "take guns away from Americans" on orders from the Clinton Administration; that UN equipment is being transported on huge trains and Russian and German trucks are being shipped to attack Americans; that international traffic symbols are used in the U.S. as a tool for foreign armies so they will be able to move easily through the country; that there is a plot to give the North Cascade range in Washington State to the UN and the CIA; that urban street gangs, like the Bloods and Crips, are being trained as "shock troops" for the New World Order; that military troops are lining up to invade on the Canadian border; that the Federal government has implanted computer chips in government employees to monitor citizens; that "those who want to take over the world are changing the weather"; that House Speaker Newt Gingrich is part of a global conspiracy to create a one-government New World Order; and that, on a specific date, the government is going to raid militias around the country.

ANTI-SEMITISM AND OTHER PREJUDICES

The researchers who track militias believe that anti-Semitism is the philosophical basis on which much of this movement rests. (It claims that Jews and "international Jewish bankers" are behind a repressive New World Order.) The idea of ordinary people being victimized by secret government conspiracies reflects the tenor, if not the content, of the notorious anti-Semitic tract, *The Protocols of the Elders of Zion*.

Nonetheless, the targets of the more extreme militia groups are not exclusively, or even primarily, Jews or other minorities. Environmentalists also are vilified. Most despised are government officials. The Southern Poverty Law Center reports that a court clerk in California was pistol-whipped by militia members because she wouldn't file one of their Posse Comitatus–like writs. According to the Rural Organizing Committee, elected officials on the local level have been forced by armed militia members who pack their meetings to enact ordinances they know are illegal, under threat of death. It is alleged that some county officials have been intimidated into forgoing re-election, potentially leaving the field open to white supremacists.

A few local elected officials have supported the militias. State Sen. Charles Duke of Colorado claimed that U.S. Sen. Hank Brown (R.-Colo.) is "owned" by Washington special interests. "I think [Brown] should be very careful when he comes back to the state. Most of Colorado is armed." Idaho Secretary of State Pete Cenerussa—at a meeting where a militia leader told his audience that "there will be blood in the streets" if a judge issues an order restricting access to a forest—said that Idaho "was planning to confer legal status on the militia once it reaches 10,000 members." On the other hand, some local newspapers are starting to editorialize against politicians legitimizing the militia movement.

In this democracy, we don't need private armies to protect us from our own government. We have the ballot box to change our government. And if our elected officials, at the local, state, or federal level violate the constitutional rights of individual citizens, we have an independent judiciary to protect those rights: Courts that have protected our rights as individuals even against presidents, the Congress, against governors, and against legislatures. Courts that told a popular president—Harry Truman, that he had to return the steel mills to the owners. Courts that told President Richard Nixon that he could not keep the Watergate tapes from the people of the United States. Courts that tell the Congress in which we serve that laws we pass sometimes are not constitutional and cannot be enforced.

No, we don't need these private armies to protect us from the government.

Carl Levin, statement before the U.S. Senate Judiciary Subcommittee on Terrorism, Technology, and Government Information, June 15, 1995.

Even though the quantity and quality of conspiracy theories and bigoted views may vary from militia to militia, they all share an anti-government animus. That paranoid stance—that the Federal government is criminal and that militia members are protecting the Constitution—is not to be underestimated. One possible explanation for his new phenomenon is that, since the fall of the Soviet Union and the end of the Cold War, the focus of the extreme right has been directed toward the American government. Jews are seen by many of the leaders of this movement—who share their ideology with new recruits who might have been attracted initially by issues like the Brady Bill—as the evil force behind government. These militia members are not talking about change from the ballot box alone. Many are enamored by the prospect of change through bullets, explosives, and heavy armaments. It is not unreasonable to surmise that this blend of anti-Semitic and anti-government paranoia and guns will result in tragedies such as the bombing of the Federal Building in Oklahoma City in April, 1995, perpetrated by individuals who carry their beliefs to the extreme.

RECOGNIZING THE THREAT

This is a movement with an ideology of contempt for the government, including criminal laws. It is urgent that law enforcement agencies understand the threat and begin to share strategies and information. Militia activity is not provided for by the

Second Amendment. Private militias are in violation of paramilitary training laws, state constitutional provisions that reserve the right to form a militia to the state, and possibly other provisions of state and Federal law.

In the words of Ken Toole, president of the Montana Human Rights Network, "We can't conduct public business in an atmosphere of fear." That fear is exemplified by a 1995 resolution of the Idaho legislature finding that "public statements threatening civil war and the infliction of bodily harm upon public officials are outside the realm of [First Amendment] rights." On the grassroots level across the country, the militia movement is harassing its opponents, threatening law enforcement officials, stockpiling weapons, and spreading paranoid rumors on the Internet. It is time that state and Federal officials understand not only the danger of this movement, but also, from a more parochial vantage point, that government employees across the country are going about their tasks while there are people planning just when to target them in their cross-hairs. These are individuals prepared to shoot at the slimmest indication of government actions. They may believe that the firefighter coming to put out the suspicious blaze in their barn or the member of the Forest Service counting rainbow trout in a nearby creek are part of an invasion force.

Laws must be enforced and, where not in place, enacted to make organized armed militias illegal. All people have a right to state their claims and organize in the marketplace of ideas. No one has the right to intimidate others with a choking atmosphere of fear, violence, and threats.

| "Congresspeople should not imagine that because a few persons with anti-government viewpoints are criminals, many or most militia members . . . are criminals."

THE MILITIA MOVEMENT DOES NOT THREATEN THE GOVERNMENT

David Kopel

David Kopel is an associate policy analyst at the Independence Institute, a think tank based in Golden, Colorado. In the following viewpoint, Kopel argues that the militia movement is not a serious threat to government officials or agencies. While Kopel concedes that some supporters or members of the militia movement have harassed or attacked government employees, he insists that the majority are law-abiding citizens and urges lawmakers not to overreact to media hype painting the militia movement as violent and dangerous. Passing laws designed to eradicate militias or restrict private gun ownership, Kopel contends, is not called for and would constitute a violation of civil rights.

As you read, consider the following questions:

1. In the author's opinion, what mistake have legislatures often made when faced with a potential threat?
2. What examples does Kopel give of laws that were passed due to misinformation?
3. According to Kopel, what must Americans acknowledge in order to respond intelligently to the militia movement?

Reprinted from David Kopel, "The Federal Government Should Set a Better Example: Militias and Gun Control," statement before the Subcommittee on Crime, Committee on the Judiciary, U.S. House of Representatives, November 1995.

From my own family background, people who threaten violence against government employees are particularly frightening. For most of my childhood, my father's twenty-two year career in the Colorado House of Representatives was in progress. When he chaired the House Judiciary Committee, he steered to House passage the only major gun control—a ban on so-called "Saturday Night Specials"—that has passed any house of the Colorado legislature in the last twenty-five years.

My mother served during the 1970s and 1980s as the Colorado and Kansas director of the federal government's United States bankruptcy trustee program. Before I went to work for a think tank, I served as an assistant attorney general for the Colorado Attorney General's Office, handling enforcement of environmental laws.

The cowardly criminals who killed so many innocent people in [the April 19, 1995, bombing of the Alfred P. Murrah Federal Building] Oklahoma City could just as well have killed my mother, my father, or myself. Just as much as any other citizen of the United States, government employees are absolutely entitled to live their lives free of criminal violence and criminal intimidation.

ENSURING SAFETY

It is wrong to dehumanize any class of people, and that includes people such as my family who work for the government. Persons who advocate and perpetrate criminal violence against government employees are no less wrongful as any other criminals who act out of prejudice and bigotry.

It is essential that government employees, like all other Americans, be safe. Not just physically safe, but safe to go about their lives free of fear, and free to exercise all of their civil and Constitutional rights.

As we think about safety, it is important not to fool ourselves. Far too often in America, legislatures, including Congress, have misunderstood or been misled about potential threats, and have enacted repressive legislation that has sacrificed liberty without improving safety.

In the United States, there is a long sad history of interest groups or government officials taking a few isolated incidents and inflating them into some kind of vast threat, requiring an immediate, repressive response. . . .

Today, there are many tens of millions of people who are frightened of the government, and many thousands (or perhaps more) who participate in militias. Some of them may have incorrect beliefs about the Brady Bill, or the ban on so-called "assault weapons," or the United Nations, or other political issues. But allegedly mistaken beliefs are no basis for federal jurisdiction.

Within these groups there are, as there are within almost any other group, a few criminals. Just as citizens should not imagine that because a few Congresspeople are found guilty of felonies most Congresspeople are criminals, Congresspeople should not imagine that because a few persons with anti-government viewpoints are criminals, many or most militia members or other government critics are criminals.

Let us learn from history. Let us not be panicked into hasty action that history will judge harshly. Let us begin a process of respectful dialogue and reform, not stereotyping and repression.

As Justice Louis Brandeis understood, "Repression breeds hate; hate menaces stable government; the path of safety lies in the opportunity to discuss freely supposed grievances and proposed remedies."

One of the reasons that so many people have become fearful of the federal government, and some have become angry, has been the virtually uninterrupted expansion of federal laws, at the expense of civil liberty. The cycle of misleading media sensationalism, a couple of Congressional hearings, and then another broad and intrusive federal "remedy" has become all too familiar.

It is possible to assemble before any given Congressional panel a half-dozen very sincere witnesses who will claim that any given topic is 1. An immense problem; 2. Rapidly spiraling out of control all over the nation; and 3. Desperately in need of an immediate, sweeping federal remedy.

Sometimes these witnesses are correct. But other times they are not.

We know in retrospect that the Marihuana Tax Act of the 1930s was the result of racist campaign of disinformation about the use of marijuana by Hispanic criminals. We know that the Food Stamp Act in the early 1970s was passed as a result of tremendous misinformation about the extent of malnutrition in rural America. We know that, despite the wild claims of various law enforcement administrators, so-called "assault weapons" constitute only about one percent of crime guns seized by police, even in major cities. . . .

ADEQUATE MEASURES ALREADY EXIST

Before enacting additional legislation in an atmosphere of media hype and prejudice, Congress would do well to slow down.

For example, we have no reliable hard data about how often

government employees are being threatened or attacked. Still less do we have any hard data about how often existing state and federal laws are inadequate to punish the criminals involved.

Current criminal laws do not require that authorities wait until someone has actually been injured or killed. Making threats is, of course, a crime in itself.

Nor are states necessarily helpless or unwilling to act. In no state are the people who perpetrate or support violent crimes against government officials the majority of the population. Or even close to it.

Some problems are plainly inappropriate for a federal "solution." For example, some persons—living proof of the principle that a little knowledge is a dangerous thing—have begun filing purported liens or other alleged "common law," instruments in some state courts. Surely the remedy for abuse of state court procedures is through enforcement of existing procedural rules which punish frivolous or false legal filings, or through reforms of state court systems to provide whatever additional remedies may be needed. State courts are the business of the states, not of Congress.

The spirit of the Tenth Amendment suggests that before federal legislature acts, it considers what the state legislatures, and the people of the states decide to do. For example, one group in Montana is planning a ballot initiative to strengthen states laws against threatening government officials. Perhaps the law will be carefully tailored to address local conditions in Montana. Or perhaps the people of Montana will choose a different approach. But in any case, it ought to be the people of Montana, not 535 people—of whom only three are from Montana—who decide what to do. . . .

PREJUDICE AGAINST MILITIA MEMBERS

Equating all militias with white supremacists is nonsense. Like the Los Angeles Police Department some militias may have members, or even officers, who are racist, but that does not mean that the organization as a whole, or the vast majority of its members are racists. Most militias are composed of people with jobs and families; people who are seeking to protect what they have, not to inflict revenge on others for their own failings.

The frenzy of hatred being whipped up against law-abiding militia members is not unlike the hatred to which law-abiding Arab-Americans would have been subjected, had Oklahoma City been perpetrated by the Libyan secret service. It is not unlike the hatred to which Japanese-Americans were subjected after World

War II. Ironically, some politicians who complain about the coarse, angry tone of American politics do so in speeches in which they heap hate-filled invective upon anyone and everyone who belongs to a militia. . . .

It is a sad testament to the bigotry of certain segments of the media that totally unsubstantiated, vicious conspiracy theories of the type which were once employed against Catholics and Jews are now being trotted out against militia members, patriots, and gun owners.

RATIONAL FEARS

President Bill Clinton has responded to what he calls "anti-government citizens" by asking for unlimited power to designate groups and individuals as terrorists and to act against those he opposes. That this request comes from the president who swore to defend our constitutional rights should alarm all civil libertarians. This is precisely the trend that "anti-government" groups are protesting. In trying to discredit and counter those who fear greater government infringements against liberty, the president proves them right.

Barbara Dority, *The Humanist*, November/December 1995.

No militia group was involved with the Oklahoma City bombing. Despite the hate-mongering of the media, the "need" to start spying on militia groups is a totally implausible basis for expansion of federal government powers.

To respond intelligently to the militia and patriot movements, we must acknowledge that, although the movements are permeated with implausible conspiracy theories, the movements are a reaction to increasing militarization, lawlessness, and violence of federal law enforcement, a genuine problem which should concern all Americans.

We must also remember that it is lawful in the United States to exercise freedom of speech and the right to bear arms. Spending one's weekends in the woods practicing with firearms and listening to right-wing political speeches is not my idea of a good time, but there is not, and should not, be anything illegal about it.

THE GOVERNMENT SHOULD SET AN EXAMPLE

If we want to shrink the militia movement, the surest way is to reduce criminal and abusive behavior by the federal government, and to require a thorough, open investigation by a Special

Prosecutor of what happened at [the Branch Davidian Compound in] Waco, Texas, and at Ruby Ridge, Idaho. If, as the evidence strongly suggests, the law was broken, the law-breakers should be prosecuted, even if they happen to be government employees. . . .

"Government is the great teacher," Justice Brandeis told us. Without the unjustifiable, illegal, militaristic, deadly federal violence at Ruby Ridge and at Waco, there would be no militia movement. The federal government should set a better example. If Ruby Ridge had led to a real investigation and corrective measures—instead of years of cover-up by both the Bush and Clinton administrations—then we would not be in the current situation.

Ruby Ridge and the Waco tragedies were not the fault of a few bad officials, but the inevitable result of a culture of lawlessness, militarization, and violence that has permeated far too much of the federal law enforcement establishment. When corrective measures are undertaken—as a coalition ranging from the American Civil Liberties Union to the Citizens Committee for the Right to Keep and Bear Arms has suggested—then we will see a massive reduction in the tension between millions of American people and their government.

PERIODICAL BIBLIOGRAPHY

The following articles have been selected to supplement the diverse views presented in this chapter. Addresses are provided for periodicals not indexed in the *Readers' Guide to Periodical Literature*, the *Alternative Press Index*, the *Social Sciences Index*, or the *Index to Legal Periodicals and Books*.

Against the Current	"What Is the Main Danger?" July/August 1995.
Chip Berlet and Matthew N. Lyons	"Militia Nation," *Progressive*, June 1995.
Peter Doskoch	"The Mind of the Militias," *Psychology Today*, July/August 1995.
Tod Ensign	"The Militia-Military Connection," *CovertAction Quarterly*, Summer 1995.
Michael Janofsky	"World of the Patriots Movement Is Haunted by Demons and Conspiracies," *New York Times*, May 31, 1995.
Peter T. King	"Q: Are Militias a Threat to the Nation's Civil Order?" *Insight*, September 25–October 2, 1995. Available from 3600 New York Ave. NE, Washington, DC 20002.
David B. Kopel	"The Militias Are Coming," *Reason*, August/September 1996.
Scott McLemee	"Public Enemy," *In These Times*, May 15, 1995.
Christopher Phelps	"The Explosive Rise of an Armed Far Right: Angry, White, and Armed," *Against the Current*, July/August 1995.
A.M. Rosenthal	"Recipe for Terrorism," *New York Times*, June 24, 1997.
Dave Skinner	"In Defense of the Militia," *USA Today*, July 1996.
Jeffrey Toobin	"The Plot Thins: The Oklahoma City Conspiracy That Wasn't," *New Yorker*, January 12, 1998.
Gordon Witkin	"The Secret FBI-Militia Alliance," *U.S. News & World Report*, May 12, 1997.

CHAPTER 4

HOW CAN HATE CRIMES AND TERRORISM BE REDUCED?

CHAPTER PREFACE

In 1997, the proposed Hate Crimes Prevention Act was introduced into the U.S. Senate. This act would allow the federal government to prosecute violent crimes motivated by prejudice against a person's sexual orientation, gender, or disability; it would also facilitate the government's punishment of any violent crime inspired by bigotry. The sponsors of the bill, Senators Edward M. Kennedy and Arlen Specter, maintain that bias-motivated crimes should fall under federal jurisdiction because unlike random assaults, they can damage entire communities or the nation as a whole. The Anti-Defamation League, an organization that opposes bigotry against Jews and other minorities, agrees: "The damage done by hate crimes cannot be measured solely in terms of physical injury or dollars and cents. . . . By making members of minority communities fearful, angry, and suspicious of other groups—and of the power structure that is supposed to protect them—these incidents can damage the fabric of our society and fragment communities." Moreover, the bill's supporters argue, many groups that commit hate crimes operate across state lines, which further necessitates federal involvement.

Critics of the proposed Hate Crimes Prevention Act argue that the measure would violate the First Amendment by allowing the government to punish bigoted thoughts and attitudes. According to journalist Gregory Buls, "'Hate crimes' laws give judges and juries the power to guess the machinations of a person's mind—in effect, to judge the heart. . . . By criminalizing the motives behind crimes, the government is criminalizing thoughts and beliefs, a common practice of totalitarian regimes." Others contend that most assaults, rapes, and murders—regardless of the attacker's motive—are not violations of civil rights and should therefore be handled by local law enforcement, not by the federal government. Authorities should punish criminal activity itself, these critics insist—not the bias that might motivate such activity.

As of August 1998, the proposed Hate Crimes Prevention Act had not passed. Legislators, civil rights organizations, and concerned citizens continue to disagree about the most effective method of combating violent crimes motivated by bigotry. The authors in the following chapter offer several suggestions for reducing occurrences of hate crimes and terrorism.

| "Individuals [should] take on the
responsibility themselves to prevent
stereotypes from developing into
hostilities and ultimately crimes
of hate."

PERSONAL RESPONSIBILITY CAN
HELP REDUCE HATE CRIMES

Armstrong Williams

In the following viewpoint, Armstrong Williams contends that
several measures can be taken to reduce crimes of hate, including efforts on the part of ethnic and religious organizations to
confront racism and bigotry, enforced antidiscrimination laws,
and equal access to education. However, Williams asserts, the
most effective way to combat hatred is for individuals to take on
the responsibility of eliminating racism and stereotyping from
their own lives. For example, he argues, people can choose to
avoid using prejudicial language and to work with others for
racial reconciliation and healing. Williams is a syndicated broad-
cast commentator and a columnist for the *Los Angeles Times*.

As you read, consider the following questions:

1. According to Williams, in what way was the so-called "race
   card" played by both Democrats and Republicans during the
   1996 presidential election?
2. As a child, how did Williams learn about the importance of
   avoiding bitterness when confronted with racism?
3. According to the author, how has Neal M. Sher worked to
   help Holocaust survivors?

Reprinted from Armstrong Williams, "Stopping the Hate," *The American Legion Magazine*,
September 1997, by permission of the American Legion. Copyright ©1997 The
American Legion Magazine.

D oomsday critics have become darlings of the press recently by claiming that America is headed for a racial apocalypse. Syndicated columnist Carl Rowan has augured a race war, and writer Andrew Hacker has insisted that we are "two nations" made separate and unequal by racial differences. But are these dire predictions really a reflection of everyday reality, and do they present an accurate picture?

Some evidence tends to reinforce this position. During the 1996 presidential election, the so-called "race card" was played heavily by both parties. Church burnings in the South were exploited by the Democratic Party and President Bill Clinton as an opportunity to stump for African-American voters. On the other side of the aisle, Republican minor contender Pat Buchanan made no effort to veil his xenophobic agenda, and he even went as far as to say that the Holocaust never occurred and that Jews were engaged in "group fantasies of martyrdom." Nonetheless, he was given a platform at the Republican National Convention.

CAUSE FOR HOPE AND DESPAIR

But political games aside, many would venture to say that race relations have come a long way in this country. For the most part, the lessons of the past have served us well. Yet, at the age of 38, I can vividly remember a time when people lived in fear of vicious racist aggression in the South.

Life in every era and for every person or group has always been a mixture of good and evil, joy and sorrow, cause for hope and despair. Undeniably, slavery was inhumane and unjust, but we can look back and see how our ancestors, both slave and master, were able to triumph over it.

The essence of America's success is found in a staunch belief in earning one's keep, being an asset rather than a burden to others and in observing the balance between rights and responsibilities. I learned this in my life at a young age. My beloved parents—father, James S. Williams, who departed this life in 1985, and mother, Thelma Williams—taught my sisters, brothers and me these valuable lessons. They taught us by word and example not to see life as a bitter struggle. They taught us that there is good and bad in people of all races, and that we should keep our hearts open to the goodness of others until they give us reason to believe otherwise.

There was too much love of life in our home and in our surrounding community for us to be consumed by hatred or fear. I remember once when, in the middle of the night, our barns and stables were burned to the ground. We emerged from the house just in time to see three white men running away. One of my brothers was extremely bitter about the incident, and exclaimed that he thought that the images of racist whites on television were true of the race as a whole. My father, though obviously pained at having his property destroyed, nonetheless took a very levelheaded stance. He sat us down and told us that the men who burned down our farm were not three white men. They were individuals with hatred and jealousy in their hearts. He implored us not to label or stereotype anyone based on the color of their skin. My father further warned us not to become embittered by other people's hatred because it would poison our lives as it had the lives of those three men.

BRINGING PEOPLE TOGETHER

I have carried this message with me throughout my life and have thus been very conscious of the way in which I interact with people. Many people in our society, however, have not had the benefit of such wise instruction while they were young. Moreover, our country still tends to be segregated by race and class, which prevents people from getting out and knowing each other. Thus, my efforts in this regard have been focused on bringing people together so they can get to know and understand each other.

For example, for several years I have engaged in the practice of hiring interns for my office from inner-city Washington as well as some from among the sons and daughters of the wealthiest families in America. My first requirement is that they all be qualified, and that they demonstrate the ability to handle the demanding work schedule at my company. It amazes me to watch them work together, observe them begin to respect each others' minds and talents and see them come to trust each other. This has worked so well, in fact, that we have encouraged other businesses to do the same. This is certainly one way in which corporate America can promote racial harmony.

Recently, Louis Farrakhan, who has long been controversial for his racially inflammatory remarks, spoke to a group of conservative Republican business leaders at the polyconomics [the study of political economics] seminar sponsored by Jude Waninski in Florida. While this was undoubtedly a daring move on the part of both, it follows logically from Farrakhan's pledge, made during his speech at the Million Man March in 1995, to end racial hostility and promote atonement. This is certainly a good sign on the part of the leadership in both the white and the black communities. If dialogue of this sort continues, perhaps some of the wounds can be mended. In any case, it is worth the risk to see if Farrakhan is really sincere this time.

BLACK MEN AND WHITE WOMEN

As many people are well aware, some of the most-repugnant racial hostilities have surrounded sexual relationships between black men and white women. All throughout the South during the early part of the twentieth century, there were stories of black men being killed for allegedly raping white women. One of the most famous cases in the mid-1950s involved Emmit Till, a 14-year-old Chicagoan who had traveled to Mississippi to visit his grandparents. While there, he allegedly whistled at a white woman and was subsequently abducted from his home and lynched. More recently, the 1995 O.J. Simpson trial for the murder of his white wife sparked the same sort of racial fires.

But the positive news is that people are starting to deal with these dangerous stereotypes. Recently, with the support of National Association for the Advancement of Colored People (NAACP) president Kweisi Mfume, female soldiers in Aberdeen, Maryland, admitted that they were not subject to rape by their male superiors. Although improprieties apparently occurred, they were not, as some were quick to conclude, made under harassment or duress. Many people had begun to assume, depending on where they stood on racial issues, that this was a typical case of black male sexual violence, or that the white female soldiers had enticed the males and then "cried rape." However, these women had the courage and strength of conscience to admit the truth. When blacks and whites are likewise open and honest about the relationships they have always had, then we will go a long way toward ending unfair stereotypes and suspicion.

FIGHTING RACIAL AND RELIGIOUS BIGOTRY

On the national scene, ethnic and religious organizations have been instrumental in attempting to combat the ravaging effects of past and present racial hostilities. One of the most notable efforts is the "Rebuild Our Churches Fund" sponsored jointly by the Anti-Defamation League (ADL) and the National Urban League. In July 1996, these two organizations, both of which have rich histories of battling for civil and human rights, were able to come together to combat the latest rash of church burnings in the South. This response, because of its strong message of solidarity, sent the message that racially motivated violence will not be tolerated, and that, in the words of National Urban

League Senior Vice President Mildred E. Love, "An injustice any-where is a threat to justice everywhere."

In addition, the Urban League, the ADL and The National Council of La Raza have collaborated to fight bigotry across racial, ethnic and religious lines. One of the major facets of their efforts is to "monitor the actions of public figures, holding them accountable when they contribute to a climate that fosters bias, bigotry and racism." In addition, they have outlined a six-point plan of action which culminates in a proposed *Presidential Summit on American Pluralism in the 21st Century.*

By making leaders accountable for their actions, these groups hope to integrate a bottom-up strategy of repairing damage done by hate criminals with a top-down strategy of preventing messages of hate from poisoning the well of public discourse.

PERSONAL RESPONSIBILITY

Beyond opportunity, we must demand responsibility from every American. Our strength as a society depends upon both, upon people taking responsibility for themselves and their families, teaching their children good values, working hard and obeying the law, and giving back to those around us. The new economy offers fewer guarantees, more risks and more rewards. It calls upon all of us to take even greater responsibility for our own education than ever before.

Bill Clinton, Commencement Speech, June 14, 1997.

Also capturing the media's attention recently was the role of Swiss and Argentine banks in hoarding gold and other valuables stolen by the Nazis from Jews during World War II. Because it is the plunder of an undoubtedly wicked and unjust war for racial dominance, the way in which this money is dealt with will de-termine how far the world has come in terms of stamping out the vestiges of the philosophy of racial superiority.

Neal M. Sher, a Washington lawyer who formerly served as chief prosecutor against Nazi war criminals, is involved in rec-onciling some of the issues involved in the return of money to Holocaust survivors—specifically the role of American law firms who have agreed to represent the banks. In a letter to Robert Rifkind, a partner in the New York law firm Cravath, Swaine & Moore, Sher urged the firm to "contribute fees earned from this representation to the Humanitarian Fund . . . to benefit needy Holocaust survivors." He further emphasized that, "under the circumstances, it strikes me as the right thing to do." Certainly no one should profit from the genocide of millions of innocent people and the pillage of their belongings.

The Need for Individual Responsibility

People such as Mfume and Sher and organizations such as La Raza, the ADL and the Urban League should be commended for taking on some of the toughest racial and ethical dilemmas of our time. They can serve as models for all Americans. But as much as these organizations do to advance racial harmony, their efforts will pale in comparison to what can be done if individuals take on the responsibility themselves to prevent stereotypes from developing into hostilities and ultimately crimes of hate.

We must do all that we can to eradicate this blight of bigotry.

To a large extent, this is just a matter of eradicating the words associated with racial division. In my life I have made every attempt to avoid hearing or uttering anything that even hints of racial stereotyping. All my friends know that I do not tolerate this language.

It has been several years since I have heard any type of racial slur uttered in my presence. The German philosopher Kierkegaard is credited with the saying that the "fundamental choice" in everyone's life is not the "choice between good and evil, but the choice by which we bring good and evil into existence for ourselves." That is to say, we can remove racism from our lives by simply making the choice not to invoke it.

Above all, this requires faith in God. Faith in God leads to a courage in one's self to be all that one can be. And the focus on self improvement leads to a belief in helping others to improve themselves.

For example, Rev. Robert Schuller, an internationally known pastor who was instrumental in calming the tensions in Israel after the assassination of Prime Minister Yitzhak Rabin in 1996, has had an integral role in preparing America for reconciliation and healing. More recently, he worked with President Clinton to set the White House on more solid spiritual footing—a Sisyphean task it seems—by encouraging the president to assume the role of "repairer of the breach" in America. Rev. Schuller seems to be helping the president repair the breach between himself and many American Christians who felt excluded from his agenda during the first term of Clinton's presidency.

Seeing Beyond Color

There are ample examples of people working together to remove the invisible veils that have prevented many of us from seeing beyond another's skin. One of the biggest challenges that remains is to be able to weave people of all different colors and creeds into the beautiful tapestry of American life. We must have the courage to see ourselves, not in terms of our colors, but on the basis of our contributions to this country.

To do this, there must be a reinvigoration of education so that people across the spectrum enjoy the same chances to succeed. There must be equal protection under the law so that criminals of all ilks are justly punished to allow a safer and fear-free society to flourish.

And if anyone discriminates against a person based on his or her skin color or ethnic origin, then that individual should be punished to the full extent of the law.

Fairness. Decency. Respect for others. Faith in God. Taking responsibility for the outcome of one's life. The bottom line is that God makes all of us equal, but disequilibrium occurs when we make different choices in our lives. In the interest of equality then, personal responsibility is paramount. All these things are essential ingredients in the quest to prevent hatred and bigotry from making slaves of free men. Moreover, eradicating racial differences can only happen when a generation of Americans becomes firmly convinced that race truly doesn't matter. If we believe that we are still the best nation in the world, then we have no choice but to face the challenge.

"Successful methods [of fighting hatred are] used by communities throughout the country."

FOCUSED COMMUNITY ACTION CAN HELP REDUCE HATE CRIMES

Klanwatch

Klanwatch, an organization affiliated with the Southern Poverty Law Center in Montgomery, Alabama, gathers and disseminates information about hate crimes and white supremacist groups. In the following viewpoint, Klanwatch argues that a well-planned group effort can help reduce hate crimes. Klanwatch maintains that several community-level tactics—such as holding multicultural rallies, avoiding protests of white supremacist marches, forming antiracism groups, assisting victims of hate crimes, and coordinating fund-raising events for social justice organizations—are effective ways to curb hate group activity.

As you read, consider the following questions:
1. In the opinion of Klanwatch, why should people avoid protesting white supremacist rallies?
2. Why are attempts to stop white supremacist events ineffective, according to the authors?
3. According to Klanwatch, what are some of the unique ways communities have found to raise funds for antiracist organizations?

Reprinted from Klanwatch, "Ten Ways to Fight Hate," 1998, by permission of the Southern Poverty Law Center.

H ate comes in many forms.

It can be stark—from anti-Semitic graffiti and the racist chanting of Klansmen to brutal assaults by Skinheads. It can also be subtle—from the reasoned racism of modern neo-Nazi leaders to the pseudo-intellectualism of those who claim that the Holocaust did not occur.

But whatever form it takes, an expression of hatred usually causes an intense reaction in a community.

Although some people argue that hate crimes and hate groups should be ignored, many others look for ways to express their opposition and to send an unequivocal message that racism and bigotry will not be tolerated in their community.

What follows are 10 ways to fight hate, drawn from Klanwatch's experience monitoring white supremacist groups and hate crimes and from successful methods used by communities throughout the country.

They are not the only ways to fight hatred, but they are a place to start.

1. *Stay away from white supremacist events.* When hate groups announce plans to march or rally, people are often unsure about the proper response.

It is tempting, but counterproductive and often dangerous, to confront white supremacists at their public events.

The principal reason is that violence by counterprotesters is becoming commonplace at white supremacist rallies and marches. Some anti-racist demonstrators travel from rally to rally, actually hoping to provoke violent confrontations with the racists. Others may attend the event simply to protest peacefully, only to find themselves enraged by the inflammatory rhetoric and caught up in the violence.

White supremacists are skilled at turning such situations to their advantage, gloating that the violence came from protesters, not the hate group.

In Denver, violence marred the 1992 Martin Luther King holiday when angry protesters at a Klan rally attacked each other, bystanders and police. One anti-Klan demonstrator was seriously injured by another counterprotester, and three police officers were hurt. Twenty-one people were arrested. Order was restored only after police used nightsticks, tear gas and Mace.

At a neo-Nazi rally in Auburn, New York, in September 1993, enraged protesters in a crowd of about 2,000 attacked the racists and pelted police with rocks. The crowd also chased the white supremacists' cars and threw bricks and bottles. Two counterdemonstrators were arrested.

Two Auburn residents, one a Jewish man, rescued a female neo-Nazi after she was struck in the face and kicked. Some of the counterdemonstrators threatened to kill another man who helped the woman.

Finally, it is important to remember that the media often cannot distinguish between curiosity seekers and the hate group's sympathizers when estimating the crowd at white supremacist rallies. Peaceful protesters can easily be mistaken for hate group supporters.

All this can be avoided by simply staying away. Then the event, attended only by white supremacists, will lose much of its appeal to the media.

MULTICULTURAL EVENTS

2. *Organize an alternative event.* To discourage attendance at racist events, communities should organize a multicultural gathering that encourages family participation. Ideally, it should be staged in a different part of the city, at or near the time of the hate group's rally or march.

Examples of such events include the following:

• In Columbus, Ohio, citizens created a Unity Day in response to an October 1993 visit by the Knights of the Ku Klux Klan. Hundreds of people participated in activities that reflected the city's diversity. The program featured rap music, traditional Hebrew songs, a school's Spanish choir, the city's opera and a gay men's chorus. The city used grant money to fund most of the event.

• In Pulaski, Tennessee, the birthplace of the Ku Klux Klan and the site of numerous Klan rallies, residents have countered these events by emphasizing the community's unity and its disgust for the Klan.

On the day of the Klan rally, downtown merchants have closed their businesses and staged a brotherhood march that is now an annual event.

• In Colorado, a ski resort offered discounts on lift tickets and rentals as incentives to keep people away from a 1992 Klan rally.

Some communities plan ecumenical services where people can express a united front against hate. Such services should incorporate all of the town's religions.

• In Wallingford, Connecticut, townspeople held ecumenical services in December 1993 in response to a series of hate crimes.

• And in Texas, a woman invited 35 churches to a prayer vigil on the same night as a Klan cross-lighting ceremony. "I figured prayer was what these people needed, and a whole bunch of it would be better," she said.

3. *Don't try to stop white supremacist events.* People often try to keep white supremacists out of their area by pressuring city officials to deny parade or rally permits.

This tactic is seldom effective. White supremacist groups have won scores of lawsuits on First Amendment grounds against communities that attempted to block their public events.

Ultimately, the event will be held anyway, and the furor surrounding attempts to stop it will only gain more publicity for the hate group.

4. *Place ads in the local newspaper.* When hate crimes occur, citizens should consider buying an advertisement in the local newspaper.

The ad should emphasize unity and support for the crime victim as well as the target group to which the victim belongs. It should also convey the message that hate crimes will not be tolerated in the community.

Newspaper ads can also counter the publicity that hate groups attract.

These ads should denounce the organization's bigoted views and should run on or before the day of the white supremacist event.

5. *Form community anti-racism groups.* Another way to effectively oppose hate groups and hate crime is to form a citizens' anti-racism group. The organization should be composed of people from every race, religion, and culture in the community, including gays and lesbians, who are frequent targets of hate crime and hate groups.

The group should stress cooperation and harmony and discourage confrontational tactics.

Some anti-racism groups, formed in response to a particular racial incident, hate crime or hate group, have found ways to sustain their sense of unity and purpose indefinitely.

One such group, the Friendly Supper Club in Montgomery, Alabama, was founded to ease racial tensions after a violent incident involving city police and black residents.

With the goal of improving the city's strained race relations, black and white residents began meeting over dinner at an inexpensive restaurant to discuss issues affecting the city. There was only one rule—each guest was asked to bring a person of another race to dinner. The Friendly Supper Club has been active since 1983.

6. *Respond quickly to hate crimes with a show of unity.* Concerned citizens should quickly put aside racial, cultural and religious differences and band together to fight the effects of hate crime on

a community.

In some areas, non-Jews have joined their Jewish neighbors to scrub swastikas and graffiti off synagogues. Elsewhere, white and black residents have gathered at black churches to remove racial slurs and to rebuild black churches burned by racists.

COMMUNITY EFFORTS TO DISMANTLE RACISM

We need to create public dialogues to move beyond polite and empty words, beyond slogans and accusations, and beyond the fears and hurts that close us off one from another. We must remember, however, that community dialogue is not an end in itself. It is an important and necessary beginning. Our goal is to move people along the continuum from uninformed to informed, from informed to concerned, and from concerned to active.

As a nation, we suffer from what Cornel West has called a "weak will to justice." In our experience, effective community dialogue can be a way both to demonstrate and to strengthen our will to become active in the task of dismantling racism. If we choose to invest the care and the time to organize the dialogue well, and if we decide to speak and to listen in a spirit of openness and trust, we can find avenues to join with one another to confront and dismantle racism in our own communities.

Andrea Ayvazian and Beverly Daniel Tatum, *Sojourners*, January/February 1996.

In mostly white Castro Valley, California, residents organized a unity march in September 1993 after a black teacher's car was vandalized with Klan slogans.

In February 1997, in response to a spate of vicious hate activity on the California State University campus at San Marcos, university employees committed to making donations to an antiracist organization each time such activity occurs. They made their first donation to the Southern Poverty Law Center.

And in Palm Springs, California, a group of high school students wore ribbons they had made to symbolize unity following a brawl between blacks and Hispanics in October 1993.

"We're trying to show the students who are causing a problem that we're not going to stand by and let that happen," the school's student body president said. "If enough people come together, we can overcome this."

HELPING THE VICTIMS OF HATE CRIMES

7. *Focus on victim assistance.* Hate crime victims often feel isolated, so it is important to let them know that their community cares

about them.

"Network of Neighbors," a volunteer organization formed in 1992 in Pittsburgh, Pennsylvania, offers emotional support to hate crime victims.

Commander Gwen Elliott, head of the Pittsburgh police department's hate crime unit, said the group offers a much-needed service.

"A lot of times, (hate crime victims) don't know how the court system works. They need support and help in dealing with their anger, so they don't go out and do something irrational," Elliott said.

Since hate crimes are not often solved quickly, volunteers should encourage victims to be patient and cooperative with law enforcement officers handling the investigation.

8. *Research hate crime laws in your community and state.* Some states and cities have broad hate crime laws that cover a wide range of incidents. Others have limited statutes that allow only data collection or cover only specific acts of vandalism.

In many states, if a bias crime is prosecuted under a hate crime statute, additional prison time or stiffer fines can be imposed.

Five states have no hate crime laws. In those states, a racial slur written on a black family's house is treated as simple vandalism.

If a community does not have a hate crime law or the existing statute is weak, citizens should urge their elected officials to support strong bias crime legislation.

9. *Encourage multicultural education in local schools.* Because more than half of all hate crimes are committed by young people ages 15 to 24, schools should be encouraged to join the fight against hate.

One way is to offer multicultural materials and courses to young people. Educators have learned that once differences are explained, fear and bias produced by ignorance are diminished.

Many schools are already teaching students to understand and respect differences in race, religion, sexual orientation and culture.

The Southern Poverty Law Center's Teaching Tolerance Project provides educators with workable strategies and ready-to-use materials to help promote tolerance and understanding.

10. *Find unique ways to show opposition.* It is important to remember that there is no single right way to fight hate, nor is there any one list, including the one here, of surefire approaches that will work in every community.

The suggested responses in this viewpoint should be adapted to local circumstances, and community leaders should always be open to fresh approaches to fighting hate.

With a little imagination, many people have found unique, and often humorous, ways to voice their opposition to bigotry and racism in their communities.

Some recent examples include the following:

• In Connecticut, a community distributed anti-Klan bumper stickers reading, "Our Town is United Against the Klan."

• In Lafayette, Louisiana, the editors of the *Times of Acadiana* said they "felt terrible" about running an advertisement placed by a local chapter of the Ku Klux Klan. So they decided to split the proceeds from the $900 Klan ad between two of the hate group's archenemies—the National Association for the Advancement of Colored People (NAACP) and the Southern Poverty Law Center's Klanwatch Project.

Bayou Knights Grand Dragon Roger Harris apparently found the approach a little hard to take. "I have to swallow hard. I really do," Harris said.

• In Springfield, Illinois, a couple gave the Louisiana idea a local twist by turning a January 1994 Klan rally into a fundraising event for three of the Klan's foes—the NAACP, the Anti-Defamation League and the Southern Poverty Law Center.

Based on the adage, "When life gives you a lemon, make lemonade," the event, lightheartedly dubbed Project Lemonade, was modeled after the common walkathon.

The project's donors pledged money for each minute the Klan rally lasted. The longer the rally, the more money was raised for the three anti-racism groups. The project's creators, Bill and Lindy Seltzer, said that the response was excellent and that pledges were collected from throughout the state.

Hate crimes and hate group activity touch everyone in a community.

For that reason, people of good will must take a stand to ensure that hatred cannot flourish.

As German Pastor Martin Niemoller said:

In Germany they first came for the Communists and I didn't speak up because I wasn't a Communist. Then they came for the Jews, and I didn't speak up because I wasn't a Jew. Then they came for the trade unionists, and I didn't speak up because I wasn't a trade unionist. Then they came for the Catholics, and I didn't speak up because I was a Protestant.

Then they came for me—and by that time no one was left to speak up.

"We must resolve that anarchistic radicalism—be it from the left or the right—will not prevail in our freedom-loving democracy."

ANTITERRORISM LEGISLATION WILL REDUCE TERRORISM

Orrin Hatch

A 1995 counterterrorism bill sponsored by Senators Orrin Hatch and Robert Dole was drafted to help reduce the incidence of foreign and domestic terrorism. This bill was introduced partially in response to the 1995 bombing of a federal building in Oklahoma City, ostensibly carried out by people affiliated with extremist right-wing groups. A revised and amended version of this bill, the Antiterrorism Act, was signed into law in April 1996. In the following viewpoint, Orrin Hatch argues in favor of the 1995 antiterrorism bill. This bill, he points out, would strengthen federal authority to investigate terrorist threats, make plastic explosives more detectable, and allow the quick deportation of alien terrorists. Such measures would protect American citizens by limiting the frequency of international and domestic terrorism, the author contends. Hatch is a Republican senator from Utah. This viewpoint is excerpted from his speech before the Senate on May 29, 1995.

As you read, consider the following questions:

1. What additional right would victims of terrorism have under the proposed antiterrorism legislation, according to the author?
2. According to the Dole-Hatch Terrorism Prevention bill, what three conditions would be required to allow a special deportation of an alien?

Reprinted from Orrin Hatch's remarks upon submission of the Dole-Hatch Counter-terrorism Bill to the U.S. Senate, May 29, 1995.

The Dole-Hatch Comprehensive Terrorism Prevention Act of 1995 represents a landmark, bipartisan effort to address an issue of grave national importance—the prevention and punishment of acts of domestic and international terrorism. This legislation adds important tools to the government's fight against terrorism, and does so in a temperate manner that is protective of civil liberties. I believe this bill is the most comprehensive antiterrorism bill ever considered in the Senate.

INCREASED PENALTIES FOR TERRORISM

This legislation increases the penalties for acts of foreign and domestic terrorism, including the use of weapons of mass destruction, attacks on officials and employees of the United States, and conspiracy to commit terrorist acts.

It gives the president enhanced tools to use his foreign policy powers to combat terrorism overseas, and it gives those of our citizens harmed by the terrorist acts of outlaw states the right to sue their attackers in our courts.

Our bill provides a constitutional mechanism to the government to deport aliens suspected of engaging in terrorist activity without divulging our national security secrets.

It also includes a provision that constitutionally limits the ability of foreign terrorist organizations to raise funds in the United States.

Our bill also provides measured enhancements to the authority of federal law enforcement to investigate terrorist threats and acts. In addition to giving law enforcement the legal tools they need to do the job, our bill also authorizes increased resources for law enforcement to carry out its mission. The bill provides $1.6 billion over five years for an enhanced antiterrorism effort at the federal and state levels.

The bill also implements the convention on the marking of plastic explosives. It requires that the makers of plastic explosives make the explosives detectable.

Finally, the bill appropriately reforms habeas corpus. Habeas corpus allows those convicted of brutal crimes, including terrorism, to delay the imposition of just punishment for years.

ENHANCING SAFETY WHILE RETAINING LIBERTY

Several points, however, should be addressed. I have long opposed the unchecked expansion of federal authority, and will continue to do so. Still, the federal government has a legitimate role to play in our national life and in law enforcement. In particular, the federal government has an obligation to protect all of our citizens from serious criminal threats emanating from abroad or that involve a national interest.

We must nevertheless remember that our response to terrorism carries with it the grave risk of impinging on the rights of free speech, assembly, petition for the redress of grievances, and the right to keep and bear arms. We cannot allow this to happen. It would be cruel irony if, in response to the acts of evil and misguided men hostile to our government, we stifled true debate on the proper role of that government.

The legislation enhances our safety without sacrificing the liberty of American citizens. Each of the provisions of this bill strikes a careful balance between necessary vigilance against the terrorist threat and preserving our cherished freedom. Several of the provisions deserve special mention.

WHAT ABOUT UNLAWFUL ALIENS?

First, I would like to discuss the Alien Terrorist Removal Act. I firmly believe that it is time to give our law enforcement and courts the tools they need to quickly remove alien terrorists from our midst without jeopardizing national security or the lives of law enforcement personnel.

This provision provides the Justice Department with a mechanism to do this. It allows for a special deportation hearing and *in camera, ex parte* review by a special panel of federal judges when the disclosure in open court of government evidence would pose a threat to national security.

Sound policy dictates that we take steps to ensure that we deport alien terrorists without disclosing to them and their partners our national security secrets. The success of our counterterrorist efforts depends on the effective use of classified information used to infiltrate foreign terrorist groups. We cannot afford to turn over these secrets in open court, jeopardizing both the future success of these programs and the lives of those who carry them out.

Some raise heart-felt concerns about the precedence of this provision. I believe their opposition is sincere, and I respect their views. Yet, these special proceedings are not criminal proceedings for which the alien will be incarcerated. Rather, the result will simply be the removal of these aliens from U.S. soil—that is all.

Americans are a fair people. Our nation has always emphasized that its procedures be just and fair. And the procedures in this bill are in keeping with that tradition. The Special Court would have to determine that:

156

1. the alien in question was an alien terrorist;
2. an ordinary deportation hearing would pose a security risk; and
3. the threat by the alien's physical presence is grave and immediate.

The alien would be provided with counsel, given all information which would not pose a risk if disclosed, would be provided with a summary of the evidence, and would have the right of appeal. Still, in our effort to be fair, we must not provide to terrorists and to their supporters abroad the informational means to wreak more havoc on our society. This provision is an appropriate means to ensure that we do not.

Second, this bill includes provisions making it a crime to knowingly provide material support to the terrorist functions of foreign groups designated by a presidential finding to be engaged in terrorist activities.

EXPOSED HEARTLAND

Reprinted by permission of Chuck Asay and Creators Syndicate.

Nothing in the Dole-Hatch version of this provision prohibits the free exercise of religion or speech, or impinges on the freedom of association. Moreover, nothing in the Constitution provides the right to engage in violence against fellow citizens. Aiding and financing terrorist bombings is not constitutionally protected activity. Additionally, I have to believe that honest donors to any organization would want to know if their contributions were being used for such scurrilous purposes. . . .

The Comprehensive Terrorism Prevention Act of 1995 provides for numerous other needed improvements in the law to fight the scourge of terrorism, including the authorization of additional appropriations—nearly $1.6 billion—to law enforcement to beef up counterterrorism efforts and increasing the maximum rewards permitted for information concerning international terrorism.

The people of the United States and around the world must know that terrorism is an issue that transcends politics and political parties. Our resolve in this matter must be clear: Our response to the terrorist threat, and to acts of terrorism, will be certain, swift, and unified.

Ours is a free society. Our liberties, the openness of our institutions, and our freedom of movement are what make America a nation we are willing to defend. These freedoms are cherished by virtually every American.

We must now redouble our efforts to combat terrorism and to protect our citizens. A worthy first step is the enactment of these sound provisions to provide law enforcement with the tools to fight terrorism.

PROTECTING THE TRUE AMERICANS

In closing, what is shocking to so many of us is the apparent fact that those responsible for the [1995] Oklahoma atrocity are U.S. citizens. To think that Americans could do this to one another! Yet, these killers are not true Americans—not in my book. Americans are the men, women, and children who died under a sea of concrete and steel. Americans are the rescue workers, the volunteers, the law enforcement officials, and investigators who are cleaning up the chaos in Oklahoma City. The genuine Americans are the overwhelming majority of us who will forever reel at the senselessness and horror of April 19, 1995.

It falls on all of us, as Americans in heart and spirit, to condemn this sort of political extremism and to take responsible steps to limit the prospect for its recurrence. Can Congress pass legislation that will guarantee an end to domestic and international terrorism? We cannot.

Nevertheless, Congress has a responsibility to minimize the prospect that something like this can happen again. We must resolve that anarchistic radicalism—be it from the left or the right—will not prevail in our freedom-loving democracy. The rule of law and popular government will prevail.

"Legislation of this kind does nothing
to combat armed right-wing
terrorism in America."

ANTITERRORISM LEGISLATION WILL NOT REDUCE TERRORISM

David Finkel

In the following viewpoint, David Finkel argues against the passage of a counterterrorism bill that was introduced into Congress after the 1995 bombing of a federal building in Oklahoma City. This bill was eventually amended, revised, and signed into law as the 1996 Antiterrorism Act. According to Finkel, the proposed bill would limit the rights of U.S. citizens and immigrants to support organizations unpopular with the government, authorize federal wiretappings and investigations without evidence of criminal activity, and allow the deportation or detention of noncriminal aliens. At the same time, Finkel contends, this bill would do nothing to stop the dangerous activities of the far right in the United States. Public exposure of extreme right-wing groups and strong support of civil liberties and democratic rights would more effectively combat terrorism, he concludes. Finkel is an editor of *Against the Current*, a bimonthly socialist magazine.

As you read, consider the following questions:

1. According to Finkel, who did the media initially blame for the 1995 bombing of a federal building in Oklahoma City?
2. What incidents does the author cite as evidence of the FBI's past inability to stop domestic right-wing and racist violence?
3. How would the proposed counterterrorism legislation criminalize support for certain international liberation movements, according to Finkel?

Reprinted, by permission, from David Finkel, "What Is Bill Clinton's 'Counterterrorism' Campaign All About?" *Independent Politics*, July/August 1995.

B lood was still literally dripping from the Federal building in Oklahoma City when the establishment's response began to emerge. The machinery went into motion for a fully fledged hate campaign against Middle Easterners, on a far bigger scale than we saw during the 1990–91 Persian Gulf crisis.

Within hours of the April 19, 1995 blast, network media were already parading their assortment of worthless talking heads always on standby for such an occasion. The bomb, they unanimously pronounced on the basis of their expert knowledge, was unmistakably a highly sophisticated device which would surely have required the connivance of a foreign intelligence service.

The worst of the lot, Steven Emerson, producer of the anti-Islamic TV documentary *Jihad in America* and the leading purveyor of sophisticated bigotry against Muslims, was prominently featured. After former Oklahoma Democratic Congressman Dave McCurdy went on a local station to claim a connection between the bombing and Arab students in the area, physical assaults took place on several Arabs, including 20-year-old Sahar al-Mawsawi, a refugee from Iraq who suffered a miscarriage when her Oklahoma City home was attacked.

The timing seemed particularly fortuitous for generating hysteria. The Oklahoma blast came in the wake of the 1993 World Trade Center bombing and President Bill Clinton's earlier banning of a number of Middle East–oriented fundraising organizations in the U.S.—some of them guilty of nothing more than opposing the Israel–Palestine Liberation Organization accords.

CLASSIC RIGHT-WING TERROR

Gears shifted quickly when it emerged that the bomb was not "sophisticated" at all—large, but readily manufactured from agricultural fertilizer and fuel ingredients. What's more, the likely perpetrators are home-grown, white patriotic defenders of America and the Constitution.

Suddenly the whole country came face to face with classic right-wing terror, a phenomenon that has existed for many decades but has generally been ignored or treated as marginal—the night-rider and lynch mob sprees in the Jim Crow South, the modern skinhead movement and murderous violence at abortion clinics, occasional murders of left political activists.

What's different this time is that, in the Oklahoma City bombing, a large number of people were murdered at random in the tradition of the fascist "strategy of tension" aimed at terrorizing an entire society. The United States attempted it, with some success, through the contra war in Nicaragua in the 1980s.

On a large scale this kind of terror was seen in South Africa just before the 1994 election. The right wing set off bombs that killed dozens and attempted (through its allies like Zulu Chief Buthelezi) to foment horrible slaughters in the apartheid-created "black homelands." This effort was defeated by the momentum of the democratic mass movement, an experience with salient lessons for us in the U.S.A.

THE PROPOSED LAW WOULD NOT STOP THE FAR RIGHT

We don't yet know if the Oklahoma bombing was intended to be a single act, the beginning of a campaign, or what. But mass murder must have been central to its intent. If the purpose had been only to symbolically hit a government building, the truck could have been parked and the bomb detonated at midnight, when the building would have been empty.

It's in the context of the nature of this bombing, with its classically far-right and murderous qualities, that we must examine the omnibus "counter-terrorism" bill that the Administration is rushing through Congress. [After being revised and amended, this bill was passed as the 1996 Antiterrorism Act.] Much of its language was probably drafted well before the Oklahoma City bombing, with the intent of capitalizing on public fear of "international terrorism."

This bill would, in fact, do virtually nothing to stop the extreme right, except perhaps hypothetically by allowing the FBI easier authority to infiltrate "extremist groups." Yet during all the decades when the FBI recorded the license plates of every car parked near a peace group meeting, it failed to stop—and even abetted—right-wing and racist violence.

An FBI informant was present in the car whose occupants gunned down civil rights worker Viola Liuzzo. The FBI monitored and taped Martin Luther King's phone calls and his sex life, but did nothing to protect him from assassination!

Both FBI and Bureau of Alcohol, Tobacco and Firearms (BATF) informants had intimate advance knowledge of Klan and Nazi plans for the massacre of anti-Klan marchers in Greensboro, North Carolina on November 3, 1979. In that incident, Ed Dawson—an informant for both the Greensboro police and the FBI—led the Klan and Nazi gunmen to the site of the anti-Klan march.

Bernard Butkovich, an agent for BATF as well as a Nazi party member, actually played a central role in organizing the Nazi-Klan alliance which called itself the United Racist Front. The full extent of Butkovich's operations in North Carolina remained obscure, since he was never called in the trials of the men who killed five of the marchers and severely wounded several others. . . .

AN ATTACK ON DISSENT

The Clinton Administration would allow the revival of this and other infamous abuses. What this monstrous legislation would do, as summarized in a release from the American Civil Liberties Union (ACLU), is to:

"Allow the government to deport aliens who have been convicted of no crime, based on information known only to the government;

"Grant to the President the power to freeze the assets of, and bar contributions to, unpopular organizations proclaimed by the President to be 'detrimental to the interests of the United States,' and bar judicial review of such actions;

"Allow the government to deport aliens who contribute to the legal, non-violent, even charitable activities of organizations or governments that are unpopular with the U.S. government;

"Subject U.S. citizens to lengthy prison sentences and fines for contributing to the legal, non-violent, even charitable activities of organizations or governments unpopular with the U.S. government, unless they first meet extraordinarily onerous licensing requirements;

"Expand federal wiretapping activity in clear violation of the Fourth Amendment; permit FBI investigations that are not based on evidence of criminal activity;

"Allow the permanent detention of aliens who have been convicted of no crime; and violate the fundamental protection of equal protection of the law by making aliens, but not citizens who engage in the very same conduct, responsible for a wide range of federal crimes."

Had this kind of legislation been on the books for the past 20 years, it could likely have been used to criminalize fundraising and advocacy for the Irish Republican cause or for the Salvadoran popular and revolutionary movement; to deport the LA Nine (eight Palestinians and a Kenyan targeted by the Reagan-Bush administrations for their support of the Popular Front for the Liberation of Palestine) as well as numerous other Palestinians; or going back further, to prosecute antiwar activists who had contacts with North Vietnamese or National Liberation Front leaders during the Vietnam War.

Legislation of this kind does nothing to combat armed right-wing terrorism in America, nor is it intended to. In fact, by targeting immigrants and supporters of a number of international movements, it will serve to implement a part of the right wing's own program, and help legitimize the political culture that spawns the fascistic groups of the extreme right.

AN EFFECTIVE RESPONSE

If Clinton's "counter-terrorism" program is actually as big a menace as the fascistic terrorism it purports to combat (in fact, it is a greater menace), then what are the elements of an effective and democratic response?

First and most important is the work of publicly exposing just who the armed far right is, and what it stands for. The present moment offers a unique opportunity for this, because of the fact that the victims of the Oklahoma City bombing were ordinary people, randomly selected. This reality brings home for the first time to tens of millions of Americans that this armed extreme right is a threat to them.

Chris Britt. Reprinted by permission of Copley News Service.

This means that the extreme-right, self-declared "Patriot" movement can be isolated. We don't yet know the full extent of the conspiracy behind the Oklahoma City atrocity, but it is already clear that those who carried it out were inspired by this movement's teachings. [Timothy McVeigh was convicted and sentenced to death for the Oklahoma City bombing. Terry Nichols was found guilty of conspiracy and manslaughter in the bombing, and was sentenced to life in prison.]

No matter how twisted they may be as individuals, they must have sensed some social wind in their sails—that some segment of society would sympathize with their action. That illusion did have a material basis: by cloaking themselves in the populist mantle of hostility to intrusive government, the leadership of the far right has succeeded in creating a semi-organized periphery, e.g. the "militia" movement and its sympathizers.

Now, because Oklahoma City reveals the true face of the extreme right, a mass revulsion against these types can strip away much of that periphery. The crisis of the "militia" milieu was revealed when the head of the Michigan Militia was ousted after claiming that the Oklahoma bombing was committed by the Japanese government (in retaliation for the Tokyo subway poison gas attack, which he said was committed by the CIA!).

A May 13, 1995 "Gunstock" rally outside Detroit was attended by a couple thousand people, a fraction of the mass turnout its organizers had advertised.

There are deeper implications. Even though almost everyone reviles the firebombing of abortion clinics and the killing of abortion providers, it's tragic that so few people in this country have seen these outrages as attacks on *themselves*. Yet these attacks reflect the same politics, the same inspiration, the same fanatical hatreds as the Oklahoma bombing.

Few heterosexuals feel personally, viscerally threatened when lesbians and gay men are beaten or killed. Too few white U.S. citizens feel the chill of personal fear when vigilantes assault immigrants. Here again, Oklahoma City could change the consciousness of many millions of people—if progressive voices are effective in making the connections.

DEFEND DEMOCRATIC RIGHTS

Second, it must be the left that consistently defends civil liberties and democratic rights. This includes, of course, the rights of expression and fundraising for Irish Republican, Palestinian and other liberation movements. Shutting down the rights of those movements in this country is the first step toward choking off domestic dissent. The Clinton bill goes further in this direction than the Bush, Reagan and Nixon administrations, with their police-state aspirations, even dared to dream of!

Defense of these rights also includes the rights of expression for views that we on the left find repugnant. It is crucial to insist on the distinction between the expression of *opinion* and organizing or carrying out *acts* of violent intimidation. This includes freedom of expression for the purveyors of right-wing paranoid conspiracy theorists, peddlers of idiotic racist arguments about I.Q. (which are promulgated more by distinguished professors than by the "militias"), and holocaust deniers—which can be defeated not by suppression but by open debate and exposure.

A positive example is the way the pro-choice movement fought for Federal Access to Clinics legislation, making sure that the bill criminalizes the blockading of medical facilities while protecting the rights of antichoice zealots to non-violent picketing and protest. So far this legislation has proven to be an effective tool for the abortion rights movement, while not giving our opponents the high road of defending free speech.

ANSWER THE RIGHT WING

Third and most important, the left—particularly socialists—must present specific answers and broad alternatives to the right wing and to Clinton-type neoliberalism.

We must stand up to defend affirmative action and other hard-won civil rights gains. Rather than accept the logic of slashing medical care, social security and welfare, we must stand up for *universal entitlements* for everyone to guaranteed health care, housing, employment, child care, education and equality.

Unlike the Republican hypocrites in Congress (and Clinton), we can offer a program to cut spending and the tax burden on working people—through eliminating the permanent war economy, through making the one percent of wealthiest people pay their share and through a massive rebuilding program for the cities, to be democratically controlled by those who live there.

The heart of the socialist program, after all, is not "Big Government" but rather working class organization, the militant defense and extension of democratic rights, and just plain common sense. It's exactly this that society cannot get from right-wing conspiracy theories, Rush Limbaugh, Newt Gingrich, Bill Clinton or either capitalist political party. The time is now.

"Narrow restrictions on speech that
expressly advocates illegal,
murderous violence in messages to
mass audiences probably should not
be taken to offend the First
Amendment."

RESTRICTIONS ON VIOLENT SPEECH WOULD REDUCE DOMESTIC TERRORISM

Cass R. Sunstein

Speech promoting murderous violence that is addressed to large audiences should be illegal and punishable, argues Cass R. Sunstein in the following viewpoint. Although current regulations protect most expressions of political dissent that advocate violating the law, the U.S. government should have the right to stop speech that encourages the unlawful use of force to kill people, Sunstein contends. Such restrictions on violent speech are especially necessary in an age of mass communications, he maintains, when information can be easily and quickly disseminated to large groups of people. Sunstein, a law professor at the University of Chicago, is the author of *Democracy and the Problem of Free Speech*.

As you read, consider the following questions:

1. According to the author, what was the outcome of *Brandenburg v. Ohio*?
2. Other than placing restrictions on violent speech, what three additional suggestions does Sunstein offer in defense of civility?
3. How can political abstractions lead to violence, in Sunstein's opinion?

Reprinted, by permission of *The American Prospect*, from Cass R. Sunstein, "Is Violent Speech a Right?" *The American Prospect*, Summer 1995. Copyright ©1995, New Prospect, Inc.

In the spring of 1995, talk-show host G. Gordon Liddy, speaking on the radio to millions of people, explained how to shoot agents of the Bureau of Alcohol, Tobacco, and Firearms: "Head shots, head shots. . . . Kill the sons of bitches." Later he said, "Shoot twice to the belly and if that does not work, shoot to the groin area."

A SECOND AMERICAN REVOLUTION?

On March 23, 1995, the full text of the *Terrorist's Handbook* was posted on the Internet, including instructions on how to make a bomb (the same bomb, as it happens, that was used in Oklahoma City). By the time of the Oklahoma bombing on April 19, 1995, three more people had posted bomb-making instructions, which could also be found on the Internet in the *Anarchist's Cookbook*. On the National Rifle Association's Internet "Bullet 'N' Board," someone calling himself "Warmaster" explained how to make bombs using baby-food jars. Warmaster wrote, "These simple, powerful bombs are not very well known, even though all the materials can be easily obtained by anyone (including minors)." After the Oklahoma bombing, an anonymous notice was posted to dozens of Usenet news groups, listing all the materials in the Oklahoma City bomb, explaining why the bomb allegedly did not fully explode, and exploring how to improve future bombs.

Fifty hate groups are reported to be communicating on the Internet, sometimes about conspiracies and (by now this will come as no surprise) formulas for making bombs. On shortwave radio, people talk about bizarre United Nations plots and urge that "the American people ought to go there bodily, rip down the United Nations building and kick those bastards right off our soil." Early in 1995 Rush Limbaugh, who does not advocate violence, said to his audience, "The second violent American revolution is just about, I got my fingers about a fourth of an inch apart, is just about that far away. Because these people are sick and tired of a bunch of bureaucrats in Washington driving into town and telling them what they can and can't do."

In the wake of the tragedy in Oklahoma City, a national debate has erupted about speech counseling violence or inciting hatred of public officials. Of course, we do not know whether such speech had any causal role in the Oklahoma City bombing. But new technologies have put the problem of incendiary speech into sharp relief. It is likely, perhaps inevitable, that hateful and violent messages carried over the airwaves and the Internet will someday, somewhere, be responsible for acts of violence. This is simply a statement of probability; it is not an excuse for violence. Is that probability grounds for restricting such speech? Would restrictions on speech advocating violence or showing how to engage in violent acts be acceptable under the First Amendment? Aside from legal restrictions, what measures are available to the nation's leaders and private citizens to discourage incendiary hate and promote the interests of mutual respect and civility?

THE LIMITS OF PROTECTED SPEECH

Recent events should not be a pretext for allowing the government to control political dissent, including extremist speech and legitimate hyperbole. But narrow restrictions on speech that expressly advocates illegal, murderous violence in messages to mass audiences probably should not be taken to offend the First Amendment.

For most of American history, the courts held that no one has a right to advocate violations of the law. They ruled that advocacy of crime is wholly outside of the First Amendment—akin to a criminal attempt and punishable as such. Indeed, many of the judges revered as the strongest champions of free speech believed that express advocacy of crime was punishable. Judge Learned Hand, in his great 1917 opinion in *Masses v. United States*, established himself as a true hero of free speech by saying that even dangerous dissident speech was generally protected against government regulation. But Hand himself conceded that government could regulate any speaker who would "counsel or advise a man" to commit an unlawful act.

In the same period the Supreme Court concluded that government could punish all speech, including advocacy of illegality, that had a "tendency" to encourage illegality. Justices Oliver W. Holmes and Louis O. Brandeis, the dissenters from this pro-censorship conclusion, took a different approach, saying that speech could be subjected to regulation only if it was likely to produce imminent harm; thus they originated the famous "clear and present danger" test. But even Holmes and Brandeis suggested that the government could punish speakers who had the explicit intention of encouraging crime.

For many years thereafter, the Supreme Court tried to distinguish between speech that was meant as a contribution to democratic deliberation and speech that was designed to encourage illegality. The former was protected; the latter was not. In 1951 the Court concluded in *Dennis v. United States* that a danger need not be so "clear and present" if the ultimate harm was very grave.

THE BRANDENBURG CASE

The great break came in the Court's 1969 decision in *Brandenburg v. Ohio*. There the Court said the government could not take action against a member of the Ku Klux Klan, who said, among other things, "We're not a revengent organization, but if our President, our Congress, our Supreme Court, continues to suppress the white, Caucasian race, it's possible that there might have to be some revengence taken." The speaker did not explicitly advocate illegal acts or illegal violence. But in its decision, the Court announced a broad principle, ruling that the right to free speech does "not permit a State to forbid or proscribe advocacy of the use of force or of law violation except where such advocacy is directed to inciting or producing imminent lawless action and is likely to incite or produce such action."

Reprinted by permission of William Bramhall.

Offering extraordinarily broad protection to political dissent, the Court required the government to meet three different criteria to regulate speech. First, the speaker must promote not just any lawless action but "imminent" lawless action. Second, the imminent lawless action must be "likely" to occur. Third, the speaker must intend to produce imminent lawless action ("directed to inciting or producing imminent lawless action"). The *Brandenburg* test borrows something from Hand and something from Holmes and produces a standard even more protective of speech than either of theirs.

Applied straightforwardly, the *Brandenburg* test seems to protect most speech that can be heard on the airwaves or found on the Internet, and properly so. Remarks like those quoted from Rush Limbaugh unquestionably qualify for protection; such remarks are not likely to incite imminent lawless action, and in any case they are not "directed to" producing such action. They should also qualify as legitimate hyperbole, a category recognized in a 1969 decision allowing a war protester to say, "If they ever make me carry a rifle the first man I want to get in my sights is LBJ." Even Liddy's irresponsible statements might receive protection insofar as they could be viewed as unlikely to produce imminent illegality. A high degree of protection and breathing space makes a great deal of sense whenever the speech at issue is political protest, which lies at the core of the First Amendment.

OLD STANDARDS, NEW TECHNOLOGY

But there is some ambiguity in the *Brandenburg* test, especially in the context of modern technologies. Suppose that an incendiary speech, expressly advocating illegal violence, is not likely to produce lawlessness in any particular listener or viewer. But of the millions of listeners, one or two, or ten, may well be provoked to act, and perhaps to imminent, illegal violence. Might government ban advocacy of criminal violence in mass communications when it is reasonable to think that one person, or a few, will take action? *Brandenburg* made a great deal of sense for the somewhat vague speech in question, which was made in a setting where relatively few people were in earshot. But the case offers unclear guidance on the express advocacy of criminal violence via the airwaves or the Internet.

When messages advocating murderous violence flow to large numbers of people, the calculus changes: Government probably should have the authority to stop speakers from expressly advocating the illegal use of force to kill people. There is little democratic value in protecting counsels of murder, and the ordinary *Brandenburg* requirements might be loosened where the risks are so great. Congress has made it a crime to threaten to assassinate the president, and the Court has cast no doubt on that restriction of speech. It would be a short step, not threatening legitimate public dissent, for the Federal Communications Commission to impose civil sanctions on those who expressly advocate illegal, violent acts aimed at killing people. Courts might well conclude that the government may use its power over the airwaves to ensure that this sort of advocacy does not occur.

THE RISKS OF RESTRICTION

Of course, there are serious problems in drawing the line between counsels of violence that should be subject to regulation and those that should not. I suggest that restrictions be limited to express advocacy of unlawful killing because it is the clearest case.

Authorizing the restriction of any speech, even counsels of violent crime, has risks. Government often overreacts to short-term events, and the Oklahoma City tragedy should not be the occasion for an attack on extremist political dissent. Vigorous, even hateful criticism of government is very much at the heart of the right to free speech. Indeed, advocacy of law violation can be an appropriate part of democratic debate. As the example of Martin Luther King, Jr., testifies, there is an honorable tradition of civil disobedience. We should sharply distinguish, however, King's form of nonviolent civil disobedience from counsels or acts of murder. The government should avoid regulating political opinions, including the advocacy of illegal acts. That principle need not, however, be interpreted to bar the government from restricting advocacy of unlawful killing on the mass media.

THE WIDER DEFENSE OF CIVILITY

What else might be done? First, nothing that I have said suggests that government lacks the power to limit speech containing instructions on how to build weapons of mass destruction. The *Brandenburg* test was designed to protect unpopular points of view from government controls; it does not protect the publication of bomb manuals. Instructions for building bombs are not a point of view, and if government wants to stop the mass dissemination of this material, it should be allowed to do so. A lower court so ruled in a 1979 case involving an article in the *Progressive* that described how to make a hydrogen bomb, and the court's argument is even stronger as applied to the speech on the Internet, where so many people can be reached so easily.

Second, the nation's leaders can do a good deal short of regulation. The president and other public officials should exercise their own rights of free speech to challenge hateful, incendiary speech. Although public officials could abuse these rights so as to chill legitimate protest, President Clinton's statements about hatred on the radio and the Internet were entirely on the mark. Public disapproval may ultimately have a salutary effect (as it recently did in the case of violent television shows), even without the force of law.

Third, private institutions, such as broadcasting stations, should think carefully about their own civic responsibilities. An owner of a station or a programming manager is under no constitutional obligation to air speakers who encourage illegal violence. Stations that deny airtime for such views do no harm to the First Amendment but on the contrary exercise their own rights, and in just the right way. Public and private concern about hate-mongering has encouraged some stations to cancel G. Gordon Liddy's show; this is not a threat to free speech but an exercise of civic duties. Similarly, private on-line networks, such as Prodigy and America Online, have not only a right but a moral obligation to discourage speech that expressly counsels illegal killing.

THE SEEDS OF VIOLENCE

The advocacy of murder is an extreme version of a far more widespread social practice: treating political opponents, or large groups of people, as dehumanized objects of hatred and fear. Too often people who disagree are portrayed as if their political disagreement is all that they are—as if they are not real human beings who have hopes, fears, and life histories of their own. Too often the individuality of opponents is hidden behind political abstractions—"the government," "the bureaucrats," "the liberals," "the radical right," "the counterculture." The seeds of violence lie in these abstractions.

The communications media sometimes help promote violence by turning people into abstractions, but they can also help to reduce violence by telling the stories of individual people. By focusing the nation on the individuals who happened to be in a federal office building one day in April, the Oklahoma City tragedy may have helped break through the abstractions that enable government-hating extremists to commit unspeakable acts.

VIEWPOINT

"Wide-open debate is the best chance for restraining violent impulses."

OPEN DEBATE WOULD REDUCE DOMESTIC TERRORISM

Virginia I. Postrel

In the wake of the April 19, 1995, bombing of a federal building in Oklahoma City, several political leaders and media commentators denounced antigovernment political rhetoric, claiming that it could feed the convictions behind violent impulses that lead to terrorism. In the following viewpoint, Virginia I. Postrel argues that these commentators wrongly compared government opponents with murderous extremists. She maintains, for example, that those who denounce government regulations should in no way be linked with antigovernment terrorists who blow up buildings. Rather than branding government critics as terrorists, Postrel concludes, honest, open political debate should be encouraged as a means to reduce domestic terrorism. Postrel is the editor of *Reason*, a monthly libertarian magazine.

As you read, consider the following questions:
1. According to Postrel, in what way is E.J. Dionne of the *Washington Post* a promoter of hatred?
2. How did Bill Clinton use innuendo to discredit his political opponents during his speech at Michigan State University's graduation, in Postrel's opinion?
3. According to the author, what percentage of Americans believe that constitutional rights are threatened by the federal government?

Reprinted, by permission, from Virginia I. Postrel, "Fighting Words," *Reason* magazine, July 1995. Copyright ©1995 by the Reason Foundation, 3415 S. Sepulveda Blvd, Suite 400, Los Angeles, CA 90034.

"Most greens can still consider themselves nonviolent for one reason: Their victims don't fight back. So far no one has taken up arms to defend his logging equipment against Earth First! sabotage or his factory against Environmental Protection Agency closure. . . . The 'debased human protoplasm' that [environmentalist writer Stephanie] Mills holds in contempt . . . will not go down nonviolently. . . . And many ordinary human beings will not give up the right to own land without a fight, complete with guns."

I wrote that in April 1990. In April 1995, it would have gotten me declared an enemy of the state, an inciter of violence, and for all intents and purposes the murderer of babies.

Which, in the eyes of E.J. Dionne of the *Washington Post* and Bill Clinton of 1600 Pennsylvania Avenue, I apparently am. After all, in *Reason*'s May 1995 issue, which subscribers received in early April 1995, I suggested that Americans are rightly afraid of government power, and I criticized Washingtonians for being too cool to use the word *tyranny* in polite conversation.

GUILT BY ASSOCIATION

Back then, it was gauche to point out that Washington rules by force—that lawmakers' symbolic gestures, from drug laws to wetlands regulations to the Americans with Disabilities Act, are enforced by government agents backed by guns. It was gauche to suggest that many government actions are unjust. It was gauche to tell Washington that the rage of the powerless was building in the land.

Now it's not just gauche, it's criminal. It makes you a terrorist, guilty by association.

"Underlying fears that the United States government is a tyranny is an increasingly popular rhetorical style that economist Herbert Stein rightly criticized . . . as 'demagogic,'" writes Dionne in a post–Oklahoma City column.

"Only a handful of unfeeling fanatics take the rhetorical excesses of politics to deadly extremes," he continues. "But the fact that they have done so—and the fact that the potentially violent militias are growing—ought to lead to some soul-searching in the mainstream. After the suffering in Oklahoma City, the country needs an extended period in which political rhetoric is toned down, words are more carefully weighed and, as the president said yesterday, 'the purveyors of hate and division' and 'the promoters of paranoia' are resisted and condemned."

As the editor of a magazine devoted not only to liberty but to rational discourse, I'm happy to endorse weighing one's words carefully. But responsible rhetoric makes distinctions, and E.J. Dionne does not.

He jumps from mad bombers to "potentially violent" militia members to gun-control opponents to anyone who uses strong language to condemn tyrannical acts of the U.S. government. He lumps these disparate groups together with few distinctions and absolutely no attempt to understand the arguments or philosophy of his political opponents. E.J. Dionne is a purveyor of hate and division, a promoter of paranoia. And he is not alone.

FROM MILITIAS TO REPUBLICANS?

In the column next to Dionne's, Richard Cohen writes in favor of disarming Americans in lieu of sacrificing other civil liberties to thwart terrorism: "Consider that the man linked to the bombing is also 'linked'"—that most elastic of journalistic terms—"to paramilitary groups that, in turn, are linked to one another. The pillar of their paranoia is the Second Amendment. . . . These are stupid people, but because they are armed they are dangerous." Using "links," Cohen can go from Timothy McVeigh [convicted and sentenced to death for the Oklahoma City bombing] to militias to Republicans who want to repeal the assault weapon ban. All in 15 column inches.

A Los Angeles Times news report by Janet Hook is direct: "[Newt] Gingrich has kept his distance from the violent extremes of the right. . . . But Gingrich has continued to champion the same causes as these extremist groups: criticism of the [1993] Waco siege, opposition to gun control and general anti-government themes." [On April 19, 1993, after a long standoff, federal agents raided the Branch Davidian complex near Waco, Texas. More than eighty people died during the operation. McVeigh reportedly bombed the Oklahoma City federal building in retaliation for this raid.]

Congress shouldn't investigate Waco, says a May 9, 1995, Times editorial, because "given how large Waco looms in the mind of a violent fringe, this is not the time to pour salt into that wound." The Times rightly did not apply a similar standard of guilt by association to rioters and critics of the 1991 Rodney King beating. [Congress eventually held hearings on Waco beginning in July 1995.]

Or consider the New Republic's Robert Wright. In the same column in which he exhorts public figures to avoid appealing to the worst in human nature and saying untrue things, he writes that "McVeigh and his buddies are anti-tax, anti-regulation, anti-gun-control, anti-U.N." He thereby appeals to the worst in New

Republic liberals by demonstrating that blowing up a building full of people is not very different from denouncing regulation. He then glibly refers to "the militia milieu that spawned McVeigh," although the McVeigh-militia connection appears to be 1995's Big Lie.

It gets worse. Buried in a *Washington Post* article on "extremism" and the Internet is the sentence: "Jack Rickard, the editor and publisher of *Boardwatch Magazine*, said that out of about 65,000 on-line bulletin boards nationwide, he has heard of about 300 for libertarian and 'paranoid' groups." *Reason's* Washington editor, Rick Henderson, faxed me the article with the greeting: "Good morning, fellow paranoid/extremist." With all those "links" out there, how can we expect a responsible newspaper to distinguish between, say, Nobel Prize–winning economists and people who think the government has put microchips in their buttocks? After all, they're all suspicious of runaway government power.

And perhaps there is no difference between free market economists and conspiracy-obsessed terrorists. In a leap worthy of Evel Knievel, "Republican" commentator Kevin Phillips actually manages to jump from Oklahoma City to the flat tax. "The 'wacko' factor is intensifying," he writes in the *Los Angeles Times*. Tim McVeigh. Dick Armey. No difference.

BLURRED DISTINCTIONS

If Phillips's rhetoric is the weirdest, it is not the worst. Phillips has no power and, these days, little influence. The same cannot be said for Bill Clinton.

This is what the president of the United States said in a widely praised speech at Michigan State's graduation: "I would like to say something to the paramilitary groups and to others who believe the greatest threat to America comes not from terrorists from within our country or beyond our borders, but from our own government. . . . I am well aware that most of you have never violated the law of the land. I welcome the comments that some of you have made recently condemning the bombing in Oklahoma City. . . . But I *also know there have been lawbreakers among those who espouse your philosophy*." (Emphasis added.)

"There have been lawbreakers among those who espouse your philosophy." Clinton may start with the "to be sures"—acknowledging that his nameless opponents are law-abiding and condemn the bombing—but he ends with guilt by association. Anyone who "believe[s] the greatest threat to America" comes from the government might as well be a terrorist. After all, they're on the same philosophical team.

Just who is purveying hate and division now? Just who is using wild words? Just who is paranoid, spinning out conspiracy theories built on blurring distinctions and imagining "links"?

Clinton continues: "Do people who work for the government sometimes make mistakes? Of course they do. They are human. Almost every American has some experience with this—a rude tax collector, an arbitrary regulator, an insensitive social worker, an abusive law officer. As long as human beings make up our government there will be mistakes. . . . But there is no right to resort to violence when you don't get your way. There is no right to kill people. There is no right to kill people who are doing their duty, or minding their own business, or children who are innocent in every way. Those are the people who perished in Oklahoma City. And those who claim such rights are wrong and un-American."

THE NEW McCARTHYISM

The American Federation of State, County, and Municipal Employees (AFSCME) ran an ad in the New York Times titled "The Call of Duty." AFSCME argued that "the people who work in government service are the faces of America. Serving all of us." Thus, continued the union, "Isn't it time to end the constant attacks on the people who serve us? Who knows what the twisted mind of a terrorist might think? Or do." Ah, if only the *Freeman* (a libertarian journal) hadn't been criticizing failed government programs for decades, the Oklahoma City bombing might never have occurred.

Aside from the fact that this argument is both nonsensical and self-serving, it is also, well, dangerous. What is more likely to create a climate of hate—denouncing illegal and unconstitutional practices by the State that are harmful and sometimes deadly, or covering up such practices and denouncing the people who point them out? It is, in a sense, the new McCarthyism— criticize government, and you are accused of being an accessory to terrorism.

Doug Bandow, *Freeman*, August 1995.

First he makes an amazing declaration coming from an advocate of bigger government and the recipient of public-employee Political Action Committee (PAC) money: "Almost every American" has had some experience with obnoxious, abusive government officials. By shifting the blame to individuals—it's those awful civil servants—he deflects criticism of the system. Don't question the law, he suggests, blame the enforcer.

He then cleverly moves the argument from whether government power is something to be feared—obviously not, since the problem is a few rotten workers—to whether violence against public employees is justified. Here, he lumps together "people who are doing their duty" (the Nuremberg defense), people who are "minding their own business," and "children who are innocent in every way."

SMEARING BY INNUENDO

It's not clear who advocates killing *any* of these people under current conditions. But at least in theory they are distinguishable. One can imagine circumstances under which self-defense might be justified against the first group; it's hard to conjure up rationales for attacking either of the other two. But Clinton's rhetorical mode is to blur distinctions.

And to smear by innuendo. By never specifying whom he is attacking—Who exactly claims the right to kill "children who are innocent in every way"? Who claims the right to kill "the people who perished in Oklahoma City"?—Clinton manages to call all of his political opponents murderers and then say he didn't.

He accomplished the same thing with his vague attack on "loud and angry voices." Was he talking about all conservative and libertarian talk radio hosts? G. Gordon Liddy? Or just conspiracy theorists like "Mark from Michigan"? He was in fact smearing them all, but preserving his deniability.

And he does this over and over again. Later in the MSU speech, he says to "all others who believe that the greatest threat to freedom comes from the government instead of from those who would take away our freedom [which, of course, begs the question]: If you say violence is an acceptable way to make change, you are wrong. If you say that government is in a conspiracy to take your freedom away, you are just plain wrong."

Is the issue violence? Conspiracy? Or the audacious claim that government power is a threat to freedom—perhaps, in the post-Cold War era, the greatest threat? Clinton sweeps them all together. Forty-five percent of Americans surveyed in late April 1995 told *Times Mirror* that they "think that the activities of the federal government pose a threat to the constitutional rights enjoyed by the average American." As far as Bill Clinton's rhetorical sleight of hand is concerned, 45 percent of Americans may just possibly advocate blowing up babies.

"INFLAMMATORY RHETORIC"

Clinton is sleazier, if less deft, when he speaks off the cuff. On *60 Minutes*, Mike Wallace asked whether the president had any second thoughts about the Waco raid. Clinton never really answered the question, but he did suggest that anyone who questions the government's actions is "making heroes" of the Branch Davidians.

And, he insinuated, raising such questions is tantamount to justifying the Oklahoma City bombing: "I cannot believe that any serious patriotic American believes that the conduct of those people at Waco justifies the kind of outrageous behavior we've seen here at Oklahoma City *or the kind of inflammatory rhetoric* that we're hearing all across this country today. It's wrong." (Emphasis added.) Asking that government agents be held responsible for their actions—actions that resulted in the deaths of scores of Americans—is, by association, equivalent to blowing up innocent people. Especially if you use "inflammatory rhetoric."

Many commentators have noted that Clinton can't tell the difference between talking and acting. They mean that he substitutes words for deeds, especially in foreign policy, and is shocked when his yammering has no effect.

In the wake of the Oklahoma City tragedy, we have seen a different side of that confusion—the deliberate conflation of his opponents' words with the deadly deeds of a handful of vicious, isolated individuals. Using tactics that would make Joe McCarthy sit up and take notes, Bill Clinton has sought to intimidate critics of government policy by branding them as terrorists.

THE NEED FOR WIDE-OPEN DEBATE

Such tactics must not work. Loud voices are not the same as violent deeds. Criticism is not the same as murder. Exposing government violence is not the same as blowing up buildings. It is grossly irresponsible to blur these distinctions. And those who rely on such smear tactics are in no position to lecture the rest of us about toning down rhetoric.

In fact, wide-open debate is the best chance for restraining violent impulses. Contrary to the *Los Angeles Times* editorialists, hearings on Waco would be a very good idea, especially now. Information is the enemy both of out-of-control government and of paranoia. Vigorous, open dissent is a powerful check on government excesses—and an important, peaceful outlet for citizen grievances.

Declaring those grievances illegitimate, and those citizens the philosophical allies of murderers, may make a weak president feel strong. But it won't make the grievances go away. And it won't make sleazy rhetoric any less sleazy.

PERIODICAL BIBLIOGRAPHY

The following articles have been selected to supplement the diverse views presented in this chapter. Addresses are provided for periodicals not indexed in the *Readers' Guide to Periodical Literature*, the *Alternative Press Index*, the *Social Sciences Index*, or the *Index to Legal Periodicals and Books*.

Doug Bandow	"Terrorism in America: Let's Not Overreact," *World & I*, August 1995. Available from 3600 New York Ave. NE, Washington, DC 20002.
Gail Russell Chaddock	"Taking Steps to Curb Hate Crimes," *Christian Science Monitor*, November 25, 1997.
Angelo Codevilla	"Anti-Terrorism or War?" *National Review*, July 10, 1995.
Mary H. Cooper	"Combating Terrorism," *CQ Researcher*, July 21, 1995. Available from Congressional Quarterly, 1414 22nd St. NW, Washington, DC 20037.
Barbara Dority	"The Criminalization of Hatred," *Humanist*, May/June 1994.
Louis J. Freeh	"What Can Be Done About Terrorism?" *USA Today*, January 1996.
Diana R. Gordon	"The Politics of Anti-Terrorism," *Nation*, May 22, 1995.
Michael S. Greve	"What's Wrong with Hate-Crime Laws," *Wall Street Journal*, April 21, 1993.
Jo Clare Hartsig and Walter Wink	"Light in Montana: How One Town Said No to Hate," *Fellowship*, January/February 1995.
Newsweek	"Cracking Down on Hate," May 15, 1995.
A.M. Rosenthal	"Recipe for Terrorism," *New York Times*, June 24, 1997.
Dan Seligman	"The Perfect Crime," *Forbes*, December 15, 1997.
Ronald Smothers	"Verdict Means White Supremacist Must Pay Black Family," *New York Times*, May 20, 1996.

FOR FURTHER DISCUSSION

CHAPTER 1

1. Karen McGill Lawson and Wade Henderson maintain that hate crimes are a serious problem in the United States. How do Lawson and Henderson characterize the victims of hate crimes? How do Kevin Alfred Strom and Joseph E. Fallon describe them? What similarities, if any, do you find in the way these authors depict hate crime victims?

2. Bill Clinton argues for expanding the definition of hate crimes to include women, the disabled, and gays and lesbians. Linda Bowles counters that expanding the definition of hate crimes is tantamount to making politically incorrect thoughts a crime. Based on your reading of the chapter, do you think acts of violence motivated by hate against a specific group should be considered a hate crime and subject to additional penalties? Why or why not?

3. William L. Pierce contends that hate speech must be kept legal because the U.S. Constitution does not protect people from being offended. How do Richard Delgado and Jean Stefancic counter his argument? Which viewpoint is strongest? Why? Does the fact that Pierce is the founder of a white supremacist group influence your assessment of his argument?

4. Based on your readings of the viewpoints in this chapter, do you think hate crimes are a serious problem? Defend your answer using examples from the viewpoints.

CHAPTER 2

1. Loretta Ross and William L. Pierce claim that certain groups encourage their members to act on their hatred and violence toward others, while Jack Levin and Jack McDevitt contend that most hate crimes are committed by individuals for "kicks" or for personal reasons. Based on the viewpoints in this book, do you think certain groups promote hate and violence? Support your answer with examples from the viewpoints.

2. Togo D. West Jr. claims that the army is relatively free of extremists and violent bigots and cites numerous reasons why this is so. Do you agree with his conclusions? Why or why not?

CHAPTER 3

1. How does John M. Swomley characterize the typical members of militia groups? How does Husayn Al-Kurdi describe them?

What differences do you find in these two descriptions? What similarities, if any, do you find? In your opinion, which author presents a more accurate description of the typical militia member? Defend your answer, using examples from the viewpoints.

2. Kenneth S. Stern categorizes the militias as a new type of hate group that targets government representatives and officials. David Kopel maintains that most militia members fear the government. He also asserts that the government's paranoia about and overreaction to militias prove that militia members' fear is warranted. Do you think Kopel effectively counters Stern's points? Why or why not? Explain.

Chapter 4

1. Armstrong Williams contends that an individual's decision to minimize racism in his or her own life is the strongest deterrent against hate crimes, while Klanwatch argues that well-planned community actions are the best way to curb hate group activity. In your opinion, which author's approach to reducing hate crimes is the most effective? Why?

2. This chapter lists several recommendations for reducing the potential for domestic terrorism. Consider each recommendation and then list arguments for and against each one. Note whether the arguments are based on facts, values, emotions, or other considerations. If you believe a recommendation should not be considered at all, explain why.

ORGANIZATIONS TO CONTACT

The editors have compiled the following list of organizations concerned with the issues debated in this book. The descriptions are derived from materials provided by the organizations. All have publications or information available for interested readers. The list was compiled on the date of publication of the present volume; the information provided here may change. Be aware that many organizations take several weeks or longer to respond to inquiries, so allow as much time as possible.

American-Arab Anti-Discrimination Committee
4201 Connecticut Ave. NW, Suite 500, Washington, DC 20008
(202) 244-2990 • fax: (202) 244-3196
e-mail: adc@adc.org • website: http://www.adc.org

The committee fights anti-Arab stereotyping in the media and discrimination and hate crimes against Arab Americans. It publishes a series of issue papers and a number of books, including the two-volume *Taking Root/Bearing Fruit: The Arab-American Experience*.

American Civil Liberties Union (ACLU)
132 W. 43rd St., New York, NY 10036
(212) 944-9800 • fax: (212) 869-9065
e-mail: aclu@aclu.org • website: http://www.aclu.org

The ACLU is a national organization that works to defend Americans' civil rights guaranteed in the U.S. Constitution. The ACLU publishes the semiannual newsletter *Civil Liberties Alert* as well as the briefing papers "Hate Speech on Campus" and "Racial Justice."

Aryan Nations
Church of Jesus Christ Christian
PO Box 362, Hayden Lake, ID 83835
e-mail: aryannhq@nidlink.com
website: http://www.nidlink.com/~aryanvic

Aryan Nations promotes racial purity and believes that whites are persecuted by Jews and blacks. It publishes the *Aryan Nations Newsletter* and pamphlets such as *New World Order in North America, Aryan Warriors Stand*, and *Know Your Enemies*.

Center for Democratic Renewal
PO Box 50469, Atlanta, GA 30302
(404) 221-0025 • fax: (404) 221-0045
e-mail: cdr@igc.apc.org • website: http://www.publiceye.org/pra/cdr

Formerly known as the National Anti-Klan Network, this nonprofit organization monitors hate group activity and white supremacist activity in America and opposes bias-motivated violence. It publishes the bimonthly *Monitor* magazine, the report *The Fourth Wave: A Continuing Conspiracy to Burn Black Churches*, and the book *When Hate Groups Come to Town*.

Euro-American Alliance
PO Box 2-1776, Milwaukee, WI 53221
(414) 423-0565

This organization opposes racial mixing and advocates self-segregation for whites. It publishes a number of pamphlets, including *Who Hates Whom?* and *Who We Really Are*.

HateWatch
PO Box 380151, Cambridge, MA 02238-0151
(617) 876-3796
e-mail: info@hatewatch.org • website: http://www.hatewatch.org

HateWatch is a web-based organization that monitors hate group activity on the Internet. Its website features information on hate groups and civil rights organizations and their activities.

Human Rights and Race Relations Centre
Suite 500, 120 Eglinton Dr. East, Toronto, ON M4P 1E2, CANADA
(416) 481-7793

The center is a charitable organization that opposes all types of discrimination. It strives to develop a society free of racism, in which each ethnic group respects the rights of other groups. It recognizes individuals and institutions that excel in the promotion of race relations or work for the elimination of discrimination. The center publishes the weekly newspaper *New Canada*.

Jewish Defense League (JDL)
PO Box 480370, Los Angeles, CA 90048
(818) 980-8535
e-mail: jdljdl@aol.com • website: http://www.jdl.org

The league is an activist organization that works to raise awareness of anti-Semitism and the neo-Nazi movement. The JDL website features news and updates on hate groups and activism as well as information on Jewish culture.

National Alliance
PO Box 90, Hillsboro, WV 24946
(304) 653-4600
website: http://www.natall.com

The alliance believes in white superiority and advocates the creation of a white nation free of non-Aryan influence. It publishes the newsletter *Free Speech* and the magazine *National Vanguard*.

National Association for the Advancement of Colored People (NAACP)
4805 Mt. Hope Dr., Baltimore, MD 21215-3297
(410) 358-8900 • fax: (410) 486-9255
information hot line: (410) 521-4939
website: http://www.naacp.org

The NAACP is the oldest and largest civil rights organization in the United States. Its principal objective is to ensure the political, educa-

tional, social, and economic equality of minorities. It publishes the magazine Crisis ten times a year as well as a variety of newsletters, books, and pamphlets.

National Coalition Against Censorship
275 Seventh Ave., New York, NY 10001
(212) 807-6222 • fax: (212) 807-6245
e-mail: ncac@ncac.org • website: http://www.ncac.org

The coalition represents more than forty national organizations that work to prevent suppression of free speech and the press. It publishes the quarterly Censorship News.

National Gay and Lesbian Task Force (NGLTF)
2320 17th St. NW, Washington, DC 20009-2702
(202) 332-6483 • fax: (202) 332-0207
e-mail: ngltf@ngltf.org • website: http://www.ngltf.org

NGLTF is a civil rights organization that fights bigotry and violence against gays and lesbians. It sponsors conferences and organizes local groups to promote civil rights legislation for gays and lesbians. It publishes the monthly Eye on Equality column and distributes reports, fact sheets, and bibliographies on antigay violence.

People for the American Way Foundation
2000 M St. NW, Suite 400, Washington, DC 20036
e-mail: pfaw@pfaw.org • website: http://www.pfaw.org

People for the American Way Foundation opposes the political agenda of the religious right. Through public education, lobbying, and legal advocacy, the foundation works to defend equal rights. The foundation publishes Hostile Climate, a report detailing intolerant incidents directed against gays and lesbians, and organizes the Students Talk About Race (STAR) program, which trains college students to lead high school discussions on intergroup relations.

Stormfront
PO Box 6637, West Palm Beach, FL 33405
(561) 833-0030 • fax: (561) 820-0051
e-mail: comments@stormfront.org
website: http://www.stormfront.org

This organization promotes white superiority and serves as a resource for white political and social action groups. It publishes the weekly newsletter Stormwatch, and its website contains articles and position papers.

BIBLIOGRAPHY OF BOOKS

Richard Abanes — *American Militias: Rebellion, Racism, and Religion.* Downers Grove, IL: InterVarsity Press, 1996.

Michael Barkun — *Religion and the Racist Right: The Origins of the Christian Identity Movement.* Chapel Hill: University of North Carolina Press, 1994.

Chip Berlet, ed. — *Eyes Right! Challenging the Right Wing Backlash.* Boston: South End Press, 1995.

Howard L. Bushart, John R. Craig, and Myra Barnes — *Soldiers of God: White Supremacists and Their Holy War for America.* New York: Kensington, 1998.

J.M. Coetzee — *Giving Offense: Essays on Censorship.* Chicago: University of Chicago Press, 1996.

Jessie Daniels — *White Lies: Race, Class, Gender, and Sexuality in White Supremacist Discourse.* New York: Routledge, 1997.

Morris Dees — *Gathering Storm: America's Militia Threat.* New York: HarperCollins, 1996.

Richard Delgado and Jean Stefancic — *Must We Defend Nazis? Hate Speech, Pornography, and the New First Amendment.* New York: New York University Press, 1997.

Raphael S. Ezekiel — *The Racist Mind: Portraits of Neo-Nazis and Klansmen.* New York: Viking, 1995.

Stanley Eugene Fish — *There's No Such Thing as Free Speech, and It's a Good Thing, Too.* New York: Oxford University Press, 1994.

Owen M. Fiss — *The Irony of Free Speech.* Cambridge, MA: Harvard University Press, 1996.

Henry Louis Gates et al. — *Speaking of Race, Speaking of Sex: Hate Speech, Civil Rights, and Civil Liberties.* New York: New York University Press, 1995.

John George and Laird Wilcox — *American Extremists: Militias, Supremacists, Klansmen, Communists, and Others.* Amherst, NY: Prometheus Books, 1996.

James A. Haught — *Holy Hatred: Religious Conflicts of the '90s.* Amherst, NY: Prometheus Books, 1995.

Milton Heumann, Thomas W. Church, and David P. Redlawsk, eds. — *Hate Speech on Campus: Cases, Case Studies, and Commentary.* Boston: Northeastern University Press, 1997.

Steven J. Heyman, ed. — *Hate Speech and the Constitution.* New York: Garland, 1996.

Valerie Jenness — *Hate Crimes: New Social Movements and the Politics of Violence.* New York: Aldine de Gruyter, 1997.

Warren Kinsella — *Web of Hate: Inside Canada's Far Right Network.* Toronto: HarperCollins, 1995.

David B. Kopel and Paul H. Blackman — *No More Wacos: What's Wrong with Federal Law Enforcement and How to Fix It.* Amherst, NY: Prometheus Books, 1997.

Alex Kotlowitz — *The Other Side of the River: A Story of Two Towns, a Death, and America's Dilemma.* New York: Doubleday, 1998.

Neil Jeffrey Kressel — *Mass Hate: The Global Rise of Genocide and Terror.* New York: Plenum Press, 1996.

Laura J. Lederer and Richard Delgado, eds. — *The Price We Pay: The Case Against Racist Speech, Hate Propaganda, and Pornography.* New York: Hill and Wang, 1995.

Laurence R. Marcus — *Fighting Words: The Politics of Hateful Speech.* Westport, CT: Praeger, 1996.

Charles W. Mills — *The Racial Contract.* Ithaca, NY: Cornell University Press, 1997.

Michael Novick — *White Lies, White Power: The Fight Against White Supremacy and Reactionary Violence.* Monroe, ME: Common Courage Press, 1995.

Jonathan Rauch — *Kindly Inquisitors: The New Attacks on Free Thought.* Chicago: University of Chicago Press, 1993.

James Ridgeway — *Blood in the Face: The Ku Klux Klan, Aryan Nations, Nazi Skinheads, and the Rise of a New White Culture.* New York: Thunder's Mouth Press, 1995.

Lyman Tower Sargent, ed. — *Extremism in America: A Reader.* New York: New York University Press, 1995.

Kenneth S. Stern — *A Force upon the Plain: The American Militia Movement and the Politics of Hate.* New York: Simon & Schuster, 1996.

Catherine McNicol Stock — *Rural Radicals: Righteous Rage in the American Grain.* Ithaca, NY: Cornell University Press, 1996.

Samuel Walker — *Hate Speech: The History of an American Controversy.* Lincoln: University of Nebraska Press, 1994.

Donald I. Warren — *Radio Priest: Charles Coughlin, the Father of Hate Radio.* New York: Free Press, 1996.

Rita Kirk Whillock and David Slayden, eds. — *Hate Speech.* Thousand Oaks, CA: Sage, 1995.

Nicholas Wolfson — *Hate Speech, Sex Speech, Free Speech.* Westport, CT: Praeger, 1997.

Elisabeth Young-Bruehl — *The Anatomy of Prejudices.* Cambridge, MA: Harvard University Press, 1996.

INDEX